Praise for *Psalms, Isl*

"A compelling study of the power of ancient, biblical poetry and sung prayer to express the deep cries of human hearts, to shape moments of profound encounter and recognition across religious and cultural divides, and to bear witness to the love of God in a hurting world. Dr. Sarwar's life of ministry and study has been a profound witness to the themes explored in this book—and now it is a gift to us to have the insights and convictions that have guided his ministry in written form. May many future pastoral leaders and students learn to return to the Psalms, to receive the gift of sung prayer, and to stretch beyond their comfort zones to reach out to others in peace-shaping, shalom-seeking ways."

—John D. Witvliet, Calvin Institute of Christian Worship,
Calvin University and Calvin Theological Seminary,
Grand Rapids, Michigan

"*Psalms, Islam, and Shalom* features Punjabi and Pakistani singers, songwriters, and other voices resounding as both Christian and Muslim witnesses that reverberate with comparative musicological, liturgical, hermeneutical, theological, and missiological implications and applications. Church, mosque, and academy will be resonating with Sarwar's intonations for the next decade-plus!"

—Amos Yong, professor of theology and mission,
Fuller Theological Seminary

"Dr. Eric Sarwar has done a great job by exploring a needed research issue in the context of interfaith relations. His academic contribution in this field of research is commendable. This research will help us to understand this phenomenon better and build bridges for reaching out to others in a meaningful way. It's a must-read."

—Dr. Qaiser Julius, director, Open Theological Seminary;
executive secretary, Theological Educators' Forum, Pakistan

"Rev. Dr. Eric Sarwar has produced a magisterial study of the Psalms in the context of the Qur'an. He masterfully imagines scriptural engagement of various religious traditions on the common ground of the Psalms, which leads to innovative peace-building initiatives and enhances interfaith relationships. This book is a must-read primer for anyone interested in the wider application of the Psalms from musical, poetic, historic, and liturgical viewpoints in interfaith contexts. The book will be an ideal resource for students and scholars of music, art, theology, history, biblical studies, Islamic studies, interfaith studies, as well as for lay people."

—Dr. Thea Gomelauri, founder of the Psalms in
Interfaith Contexts Reading Group;
director of the Oxford Interfaith Forum

"This book and the research behind it are important missiological contributions to interfaith dialogue between Muslims and Christians through the use of the Psalms. Dr. Sarwar 'unmutes the prophetic voice of David,' who is revered in both Islamic and Christian traditions. In an approach that is culturally relevant and contextually sensitive, Dr. Sarwar seeks a 'sur-sangam' convergence in Indic musicality and the traditional ragas form to bring together culturally appropriate Christian witness in Psalm Festivals and other opportunities for Christian-Muslim dialogue. Dr. Sarwar offers practical recommendations for continued dialogue and witness in the Pakistani context and among the diaspora. I highly recommend this book as a new and creative approach to interfaith dialogue."

—Rev. Greg Sinclair, Diaspora Ministry Leader,
Resonate Global Mission,
Hamilton, Ontario

"Lucid and highly readable, Eric Sarwar's *Psalms, Islam, and Shalom* is a carefully researched song of the heart. The long and bloody history of Muslim-Christian conflict in Pakistan would ordinarily have condemned from the start a young Christian pastor's best efforts to create spaces of dialogue and relationship with Muslim neighbors. But Sarwar's social location as a musically trained Christian leader with an unusual gift for connecting deeply with Pakistan's Muslim musicians and religious leaders opened his eyes to the treasure that the Psalms represent as a shared legacy that binds Christians and Muslims together. *Psalms, Islam, and Shalom* is the story of that shared legacy."

—Rev. Dr. B. Hunter Farrell, director, World Mission Initiative, Pittsburgh Theological Seminary

"Eric Sarwar's important work is crucial for its scholarship, certainly. However, I believe it is a paradigmatic landmark paving the way for Muslims and Christians to meet in *worship*. As such, it opens a whole new realm of possibilities that traditional evangelism and dialogue models do not imagine."

—Kevin Higgins, president, William Carey International University; general director, Frontier Ventures; facilitator, Muslim Ministries

"This book is a resource for chaplains, pastors, musicians, missionaries, and scientists to explore song's empowerment of interfaith friendship. Without blurring Christian faith distinctives, Dr. Eric Sarwar bravely probes how common musical experience opens shared and surprising meaning among people of different faiths. In a divisive digital world, this book offers practices that cross religious divides, sharing harmonies of faith as a bridge over troubled waters."

—Dr. Shirley J. Roels, executive director, International Network for Christian Higher Education

"If Muslim-Christian peacemaking requires imagination, we exclude the arts at our peril. While traditional efforts begin with interfaith dialogue, negotiation, or apologetics, Eric Sarwar charts his path to peace through the power of song. A songwriter himself, Sarwar opens up an impressive aesthetic approach to interfaith engagement."

—Matthew Kaemingk, author of *Christian Hospitality and Muslim Immigration in an Age of Fear*;
Mouw Chair of Faith and Public Life, Fuller Seminary

"Delightful, engaging, and innovative! Dr. Sarwar engages Muslim-Christian interfaith dialogue from a new and creative angle using music and common Zabur/Psalms heritage as a bridge. I see huge potential for contextual evangelism, discipleship, dialogue, and more through the Psalms-singing and music. This is a must-read for anyone interested in contextual theology, Muslim-Christian relations, or South Asian studies."

—Esa Autero, dean of Graduate Studies,
South Florida Bible College and Theological Seminary

"Rev. Dr. Eric Sarwar's groundbreaking and timely book challenges the church, not least in Pakistan, to recognize the limitations of traditional mission methods and to engage in new, creative, contextual missional approaches for the twenty-first century. In particular, Dr. Sarwar highlights the importance of 'worship as witness' as he focuses on how vernacular translations of the Psalms, composed in cultural music styles, open up a third space for creative conversations with Islam. I warmly commend this book, especially to those eager to explore new frontiers in the mission of God."

—Rev. Uel Marrs, Global Mission Secretary,
The Presbyterian Church in Ireland

PSALMS, ISLAM, and SHALOM

PSALMS, ISLAM, and SHALOM

A Common Heritage of Divine Songs for Muslim-Christian Friendship

Eric Sarwar

FORTRESS PRESS
MINNEAPOLIS

PSALMS, ISLAM, AND SHALOM
A Common Heritage of Divine Songs for Muslim-Christian Friendship

Library of Congress Control Number: 2023932329 (print)

Cover design: Emily Harris

Print ISBN: 978-1-5064-9119-6
eBook ISBN: 978-1-5064-9120-2

Contents

1

Introduction

A New Approach toward Shalom

Almost two thousand years ago, the gospel of Jesus Christ came to the land now known as Pakistan. Tradition tells us the Apostle Thomas brought the Good News to the Indus River Valley in the first century on his Great Commission journey to the Indian subcontinent.

Although some Hindus and Buddhists received the gospel with joy, the roots of the Christian faith never grew deep and wide in the Indus Valley. When Muslim missionaries reached the area in the seventh century, they conquered the land for Islam. The nation of Pakistan, itself carved out of the British Raj of the Indian subcontinent on August 14, 1947, as a place specifically for Muslims, now hosts the second largest number of Muslims in the world after Indonesia. About 96 percent of the country's 242 million people claim the faith of Muhammad, while some 2.5 percent of Pakistanis identify as Christians.

For fourteen centuries, a gap of mutual suspicion and hostility has existed between Christians and Muslims, despite attempts to engage theologically, apologetically, polemically, and militarily (such as the Crusades). During the past four decades, increased Islamization in Pakistan has led to blasphemy laws, nationalization of Christian institutions, a state policy of religious and political profiling, and discrimination against followers of

Jesus. Historic animosity has resulted in widespread violence and persecution. Amid such an environment, past efforts at reaching Muslims with the gospel have proved ineffective or even detrimental, highlighting a need for a different approach to engaging the Islamic culture.

Psalms as a Common Heritage

My research, experience, and practice have uncovered the valuable and mostly untapped role of the biblical Psalms in fostering peaceful friendship with Muslims. The book of Psalms, called *Zabur* in Arabic, is a common heritage of divine song that can be used as a point of connection for public witness between Muslims and Christians. Especially in the Pakistani context, the Psalms carry vast potential, in terms of both text and musical expression, as a bridge to peacemaking and missional engagement. Yet the book of Psalms has never been a significant part of witness to the Muslim world.

The Qur'an teaches its followers to read and respect the "previous scriptures," consisting of the Torah (*Tawrat*), the Psalms (*Zabur*), and the Gospel (*Injil*). Most Muslims, however, do not read any of them. Many do not read even the Qur'an. From a historical perspective, although Zabur is among the four revealed books of Islam (including the Qur'an itself), most of the interfaith conversation has centered around the Tawrat and Injil. Why have the Psalms been muted or neglected?

Until recently, the Church has shown little interest in using music and psalms to build a bridge to the Islamic culture. The value of these resources for missions has been overlooked not only in Pakistan but in broader Christian engagement with the Muslim world. Some, including researcher and theologian Jeremy S. Begbie, do recognize music as a powerful medium that resonates with the dynamics of Christian faith. Begbie contends that music has "considerable power to generate fresh and fruitful resources for the theological task."[1] Yet music remains neglected in the theological corridor as an abstract construct, its process of communication seen as too opaque or fluid for meaningful analysis.

Music as a Creative Strategy

Music communicates powerful information and emotion. Its emotive and spiritual language can serve as a peacemaking bridge between Muslims and Christians. When used in interfaith gatherings, music creates a mental, emotional, and spiritual bond in shared performance spaces.

Pakistan, which literally means "land of the pure," is a unique country where famous gospel singers are Muslim artists. It is an oral culture with a tradition of poetry, sacred hymns, and the oral performative practice of cantillation, affording great potential for bonding people across religious lines. Because Pakistani music serves as a tool for communication and cultural cohesion, the common sacred text of Psalms and cultural musical tunes provide a rich and robust context for religious dialogue.

This book proposes a creative strategy for building Muslim-Christian friendship by using the lyrical poetry of the Psalms translated into the vernacular and composed in culturally relevant music. The book of Psalms, I believe, provides a mandate for musical mission in the Islamic context.

My Story

As a fourth-generation Christian, musician, and pastor from Pakistan, with fluency in Punjabi, Urdu, and Hindi, I hold both cultural music and the Psalms close to my heart. They represent my identity. My grandfather, Mohan Lal, provided my classical music training in North Indian musicology. I was given the title *sadhu* (Sanskrit for "a holy man") during my initial immersion into the traditional rhythms and rhymes of Pakistan's music culture, including raga-based psalm singing. This training led me to serve as a worship leader with liturgical and contemporary worship teams in Karachi.

(In Sanskrit, raga, or *raag*, literally means "color," or "tone." In the musical and technical sense, the term raga means a combination of musical tones in successive order. According to the ancient traditional system of melodic patterns or modes, a precise natural flow or drift between notes affected by its ascending and descending scales is called raga. Chapter 3 will explore this musical tradition in more detail.)

I have been raised in the midst of religious and social hostility against Christians in my country and know the depth of distrust between the faiths. At the same time, my interaction with Muslim musicians and educators has occurred on multiple levels. I have engaged with Muslims as a music teacher for ten years (2002–2012) in Karachi's largest Muslim girls' school. I have worked with Muslim artists in the entertainment industry by producing psalms and Christian gospel song albums. Friendships with Sufi musicians grew through collaborative production of a musical album of the Psalms. In addition, I have conducted short-term music classes in juvenile prison, and later taught at the Karachi central jail.

Such experiences intrigued me and led to further exploration of how cultural music and religious commonalities can lead to engagement with Muslim neighbors in the pursuit of peace and religious harmony. In 2004, I founded the Tehillim School of Church Music and Worship in Pakistan. Tehillim is the Hebrew word for psalms, and the school has developed a missional model incorporating music and the Psalms. The music produced by the Tehillim School is used not only for the spiritual nourishment of Christians but also for Christian-Muslim combined recordings in Pakistan.

In 2012, I had the opportunity to interact via the Psalms with Sufis at their famous shrine of Shah Abdul Latif Bhittai near Hala, a city on the Indus River in the southeastern Pakistani province of Sindh. That watershed missional moment opened the doors for me to explore the role of psalms in engaging with the larger Muslim community, particularly Sunni and Shi'a Muslims in Pakistan. (The majority of Muslims in Pakistan identify with the Sunni sect; Shi'as make up about 10 to 15 percent, while the Sufi tradition has a strong and popular following among both sects.)

This experience nurtured my interest in exploring theories and extending creative bridge-building toward *salam*. *Salam* or *salaam* in Arabic is equivalent to *shalom* in Hebrew, signifying a deep and comprehensive peace and well-being. Muslims and Christians both use this word *salam* in their regular greetings, and Christians from Pakistan use the same word to greet each other. All three monotheistic communities of faith use these parallel terms for a blessing of peace in their expressions of greeting or respect to one another.

The Tehillim School began sponsoring Worship Symposiums and psalm festivals across Pakistan. In 2018, during the first phase of field research for my doctoral dissertation, I participated in interfaith psalm festivals in three Pakistani cities: Rawalpindi, Lahore, and Karachi. These worship events involving both Muslims and Christians have become a launching pad for interfaith dialogue, and will be described in more detail later on.

Sur-Sangam: A Divine Blend

The value of this approach is *sur-sangam*, a compound word from *sur* (musical note) and *sangam*, the Sanskrit word for confluence. Sangam is a concept of two rivers crossing and meeting each other. The point of confluence is a sacred place in the Indian subcontinent, as described in a famous proverb: "Those who bathe at the place where the two rivers flow together, rise up to heaven."

As I am using the term, *sur-sangam* is a confluence of text and tune that enables a gathering for the unity of souls and minds at one shared space. The concept of *sur-sangam* for Muslim and Christian gatherings is to come together at religious musical events to delight aficionados of cultural music and scriptural text. The resulting blend—of ethnomusicology and anthropology, of Muslim and Christian faith traditions, of qur'anic and biblical streams—brings together ideas and concepts with a recognition of the value both traditions bring to the dialogue. The collaborative goal is to promote peacemaking and foster interfaith harmony amidst conflict. It is a sociological phenomenon, not a theological investigation.

The Call for a New Approach

This study examines contextual musical expressions and related poetic content from the Zabur/Psalms as a bridge toward meaningful interfaith dialogue between Muslims and Christians. I propose uniting the musical imagination with the text of the Psalms and indigenous tunes as a missiological discipline to engage the Muslim world in the twenty-first century. Creative approaches toward translating psalms into cultural texts will provide common ground for Muslim-Christian engagement.

In this book, I present my personal discovery of how Pakistani musical genres embedded with the text of Psalms have been used to promote public witness processes in Pakistan. The shared spiritual heritage of the Zabur/Psalms brings adherents of both Islam and Christianity to reimagine scriptural engagement using the sacred text as a catalyst to foster interfaith friendship. In addition, the religious and cultural music of these two faiths invites research into ways for Christians to live in peace and harmony with our local and global Muslim neighbors.

Psalms in ethnic musical expression can also break the barriers of religious antagonism. Each ethnic group in Pakistan (Punjabi, Sindhi, Baluchi, Pashtoo, and Saraiki) has its distinct musical expression that can play a major role for public witness in the nation. Given the similarity of psalms in the sacred texts of the Abrahamic religions, the book of Zabur/Psalms with its wide-ranging themes presents a shared foundation for musical interfaith dialogue and transformative peacemaking processes. This approach remains largely unexplored in missiological praxis.

During the last century, Christian witness toward the Muslim world has changed dramatically as followers of Jesus strive to find common ground for conversation with Islamic peoples. Compared to historic engagements through confrontational polemics, colloquial debate, crusades, and colonialism, modern mission approaches have taken a more amicable stance. Post-Vatican Protestant scholars are drawing attention to transformational peacebuilding between Muslims and Christians through mystical and artistic approaches.[2] These developments all represent encouraging trends.

Let the Music Begin

If there is a dearth of literature focusing on the intersection of music, psalms, and Islam, I have found no literature at all relating to interfaith friendship between Muslims and Christians through use of cultural music and the text of the Psalms. My fervent hope is for my research to become an important part of the conversation in multiple disciplines. I present it with the same respectful and humble motivation reflected in Kenneth Cragg's description of the legacy of William Henry Temple Gairdner (1873–1928), a Scottish missionary to Muslims in Cairo: "This stake-peg of all his mission meant that all 'debate' or 'dialogue' was with intent to save, not crudely to score, nor idly to compare, nor cosily to converse."[3]

The structure of this book is orchestrated within the framework of a Muslim-Christian collaborative psalm festival. After this introductory chapter to set the stage, the following three parts lead the reader on a musical journey using the analogy of a classical raga performance, beginning with *Alap* (Prelude), then *Bandish* (Performance), followed by *Taan* (Postlude).[4]

The book of Psalms/Zabur can build a bridge for peacemaking and sustainable relationships of *salam/shalom* among Muslims and Christians. However, we cannot comprehend Islamic thought without understanding the role of art in the prophet Muhammad's life and how he and his followers interacted over the centuries that followed. After a brief look at the concepts of ethnomusicology, its intersection with missiology, and the music culture of Pakistan, the following chapter explores the positive and negative engagements between Islam and Christianity starting in the seventh-century Arab peninsula, with a focus on the role and perceptions of art and music.

Notes

1 Jeremy S. Begbie, *Theology, Music, and Time*, Cambridge Studies of Christian Doctrine (Cambridge: Cambridge University Press, 2000), 4.

2 See: Phil Parshall, *Bridges to Islam: A Christian Perspective on Folk Islam* (Downers Grove, IL: InterVarsity Press, 2006). Roberta R. King, *Global Arts and Christian Witness: Exegeting Culture, Translating the Message, and Communicating Christ* (Grand Rapids, MI: Baker Academic, 2019). B. Neil Woodhouse, "'You are Jesus, and I am your bird': Christ, Persian poetry, and theological imagination in the Iranian diaspora," *Missiology: An International Review*, 4 (2016): 416–29, https://journals.sagepub.com/doi/10.1177/0091829616658497. Evelyne A. Reisacher, *Joyful Witness to the Muslim World*, (Grand Rapids, MI: Baker Academic, 2016).

3 Kenneth Cragg, "Temple Gairdner's Legacy," *International Bulletin of Missionary Research*, 4 (1981):164–7, https://journals.sagepub.com/doi/10.1177/239693938100500403

4 *Alap* is a rhythmically fluid yet slow, methodical progression of notes as an introductory section of the performance of a *raga*. It expresses the emotional feel and essential notes with melodic turns of the *raga* to be performed, and it develops the rendition of *ragas* to create the ambiance and atmosphere for the specific *raga*. *Bandish* encapsulates the characteristics and syllables of the *raga*. It divides into two parts: *Asthayee* and *Antara*, which demonstrate the musical arrangements governed and guided by the *raga's* grammar. It is a melodic interpretation of the *raga* that also evokes contrasting emotions. *Taan* is a short, final, and fast-tempo melodic passage, an improvised vocal phrase of *raag* generally rendered at the end. It expands the breadth and width, weaving together the notes of the raga.

Prelude
Alap

2

From Polemics to Peacemaking

Music has been called the language of the heart. Even without words, it speaks to us. It is an emotional and spiritual language that creates a spiritual bond. Music touches deep parts of the soul, evoking feelings and memories, both conscious and subconscious. It can call forth responses that bypass the analytical mind, providing opportunities for communication not available through ordinary conversation.

This chapter serves as a "Prelude" to set the stage for the focus of this book exploring the dynamics between music and missions. An introduction to ethnomusicology and music culture initiates a discussion of the intersection of these concepts with missiology for a peacemaking process between Christians and Muslims.

Ethnomusicology and Music Culture

Everything that relates to sound and music in culture is considered music culture. Music culture is a subfield of ethnomusicology, the study of music in any given culture, including why and how human beings are musical. Initially Alan Merriam introduced the triangular concept of ideas, behavior, and sound in his monograph *The Anthropology of Music* in 1964, the seminal work that has shaped the direction and purpose of ethnomusicology.[1] He sees ethnomusicology as a hybrid study involving social science and humanities. Merriam states that human behavior, communication, and emotions are interlinked with the music of a given culture. Because music and melody have different meanings from culture to culture and place to place, this variation shapes the diverse music cultures.

The concept of *musicking* is essential to an artistic approach to Christian-Muslim relations. Musicologist Christopher Small introduced the theory of *musicking* as a collective action of a whole community present at a music event. He holds that the song or piece of music expresses the whole human activity beyond the page, and that only through performance will the multiple layers of a song reveal themselves. Small further described *musicking* as "to take part, in any capacity, in a musical performance, whether by performing, by listening, by rehearsing or practicing, by providing material for performance (what is called composing), or by dancing."[2] Clearly, *musicking* features key dynamics that can foster musical dialogue in the public sphere.

Music has missional potential, so it is important to learn to make sense of people's music found in a particular local context. In their book *(un)Common Sounds*, Roberta R. King and Sooi Ling Tan propose musical pathways toward peace and reconciliation through interfaith dialogue. They find a striking similarity of sacred texts as a point of convergence in the three Abrahamic faiths of Judaism, Christianity, and Islam. They recognize "musical interfaith dialogues: from cantillation to instrumental 'dialogues of silence,'" and find links between music and religion that "provide rich resources for understanding the belief systems of peoples and their influence on society and daily living."[3]

All three of the Abrahamic faiths attach great importance to authorized holy texts. These include the Torah (Mosaic law), the Bible, the Qur'an, and the Hadith (a record of the sayings and actions of Muhammad). In addition, poetry, hymns, songs, and cantillation incorporating sacred scriptures are also revered. In light of the contemporary conflicts between Muslims and Christians, the poetic or musical cantillation of sacred text offers significant opportunities to foster interfaith harmony. We will discover in the coming chapters how cultural musical tunes embedded with the text of the book of Psalms/Zabur can promote the peacemaking process in Pakistan and beyond.

Pakistani Music Culture and the Role of Psalms

The music culture of Pakistan is a blend of religious traditions. It reflects a diverse acculturation due to the convergences of Hinduism and Islam in the region. Classical dancer and dance teacher Sheema Kermani has described the music culture of Pakistan as "a synthesis of Christianity, Hinduism, Sikh, Sufism, and Islam."[4]

Artifacts and statues from the Indus Valley civilization dating from 2500 BCE show dancing figures and figures with musical instruments. Tracing the history of music in the Indian subcontinent is an opportunity to broaden our understanding of identity and friendship beyond religion and borders.

In contrast to the well documented, historically established, shared common heritage of Judeo-Christian psalmody, Islam as the third monotheistic faith has less documented practice of psalmody due to historic animosity and political confrontation with Judaism and Christianity. Historians find few instances where Muslims and Christians engaged in dialogue around the Psalms/Zabur. For the most part, these discussions took place in the Sultan's royal court, and served as an attempt to prove the superiority of Muslim faith in the context of armed victory over Christian territories. Such debates also show the potential for practitioners of the monotheistic religions, through understanding of common theological contexts, to contribute to mutual acts of sacred presentation.

Interreligious peacemaking in the twenty-first century demands an understanding of the Psalms as well as the musical practices of Pakistani and other Islamic cultures, recognizing these as important elements of missiological significance.

Patterns of Muslim-Christian Engagement

The fourteen-century history of Muslim-Christian relations has taken many forms of conflict and cooperation, diatribe and dialogue, hatred and hospitality. Throughout history, Christian-Muslim encounters characteristically have taken one of three forms: colloquial, collaborative/confrontational, or colonial, sometimes called the "C-encounters." Despite their oversimplification, these three "Cs" reflect the hostility and mistrust of Islamic history interfaced with Christianity.

The first C, Colloquium, looks at the historical encounters of Christ-followers with Muhammad, as well as qur'anic colloquial responses toward poetic and musical art in the Arabian Peninsula, including Christian art. The second C, Collaborative/Confrontational encounters, reflects philosophical and theological exchanges including the rise of Sufism as a parallel path for spiritual expressions during the Righteous Caliphate from the seventh to the seventeenth centuries. It also spotlights the direct confrontation with Christianity symbolized by the Crusades as invasions to establish Christian territories in Muslim strongholds. The third C, Colonialism, focuses on the colonial interactions of Christianity with Islam. This approach has been polemic and antagonistic, and therefore requires fresh models and a move away from the old methods of mission, particularly in these Islamic contexts.

We will take a look at each of these patterns of engagement.

Colloquium

Despite his aggressive attitude toward the polytheists in Arabia, the prophet Muhammad had rare but significant encounters with Christians of his time. Ibn Ishaq recorded five main occasions during the period 610–622 CE when Muhammad had direct interactions with Christians. The Prophet came into contact with Jewish and Christian communities living around the Arab peninsula but the possible influence of Judeo-Christian tradition on his inspiration is debatable. Muhammad first encountered Christianity through three sects judged heretical by the Eastern and Western churches: Nestorians, who believed that, like oil and water, the two natures of Christ cannot mix; Monophysites, who believed that, like wine and water, the human and divine natures of Jesus can mix, though in a way impenetrable to theological analysis; and Arian Christians, who believed Jesus was created, not begotten.[5]

The Syrian and Nestorian churches were present in several Arab tribes at the borders of Arabia, including Lakhum, at northeastern frontiers, and Axum, across the Red Sea in Ethiopia. In the southwestern region of Arabia, the Christians of Najran, near the east coast of the Red Sea, worshiped with their bishops, priests, and Scriptures in a Syriac language. However, the Bible was not translated into Arabic until 837 and not published until 1516.

A small community of Christian slaves, local converts, and foreigners lived in Mecca during the early seventh century. Aside from the delegation of Christians from Najran who came to visit Muhammad and could worship in the Prophet's mosque in Medina, Muhammad had little connection with Christians. Scholars have observed that Muhammad was both surprisingly tolerant of Christians and quite uninformed about the heterodoxy of Christianity.

Islam, as a strictly monotheistic religion in the then-polytheistic Arab peninsula, destroyed all kinds of visual art related to pagan worship. The reliable Islamic sources studied by modern scholars reveal that after the conquest of Mecca in 632 CE, Muhammad's army found visual artistic expressions of pagan deities in the Ka'aba, the Meccan shrine. Martin Lings (1909–2005), a follower of Algerian Sufi master Ahmad al-Alawi (1874–1934), narrated the story of what happened to this visual art:

> Apart from the icon of the Virgin Mary and the child Jesus, and a painting of an old man, said to be Abraham, the walls inside [Ka'aba] had been covered with pictures of pagan deities. Placing his hand protectively over the icon, the Prophet told 'Uthman to see that all the other paintings, except that of Abraham, were effaced.[6]

This account has also been reported by Islamic historians al-Azraqi and Ibn Ishaq, and illustrates Muhammad's respect and honor toward Jesus and Mary as reflected in the Qur'an in Surah 17 (*Maryam*). Muslim scholars, however, negate and do not accept this story since it shows favor to Christian visual art.

Collaboration and Confrontation

The medieval era from the seventh century until the fourteenth century was a time of dialogues, debates, and struggles for dominance between Muslims and Christians. The history of Muslim-Christian polemics begins in the eighth century CE, including aggressive attacks by Byzantine Christian scholars. This polemical approach to dialogue, initiated by Byzantine theologians and monks such as Theodore Abu Qurrah and Theophanes the Confessor (ca. 752–818 CE), attacked the genesis of Islam. John of Damascus (676–749 CE) opined that Islam was a heresy. On the Muslim side, 'Alī al-Tabarī (ca. 770–ca. 855 CE), Ibn Hazm (994–1064 CE), Al-Ghazālī (1059–1111 CE), and Ibn Taymiyyah (1263–1328 CE) presuppose an Islamocentric approach. Thus, both

Muslims and Christians maintained their stance of isolation and confrontation.

Amidst the polemic engagement, an alternative model was presented by both Muslim and Christian scholars. One such scholar was Cyril of Thessalonica (ca. 826–869), whose work among Arab Muslims in Samarra (in modern Iraq) and among the Khazars (in present-day southern Russia) included both Jews and Muslims. The philosopher Cyril offered five strategies to present the gospel, Christ, and the Trinity, and responded to the queries of these medieval Muslim and Jewish thinkers. His apologetic approach was based upon philosophy, shared text, adapting local language and culture, and proclaiming a Creator God.

Collaboration involved numerous philosophical and theological exchanges, while both sides also engaged in militant confrontations and invasions, including the Crusades, to establish territories for their religion. In addition, this era saw the emergence of Sufism, which will be mentioned separately in this chapter and in more detail later on in the book.

One of the early examples of theological dialogue is the invitation of the third Abbasid Caliph al-Mahdi (ruled 775–785 CE), probably in 781, to engage with the Catholicos Timothy, patriarch of the Nestorian church in Iraq. The two-day dialogue with Timothy in Baghdad was mostly theological, including an apologetic defense of the Trinity and Christology.[7]

Another dialogue/debate is recorded in the *Bet Hale Disputation* (ca. 720 CE), an early manuscript that shows how Muslims inferred and understood Psalm 37:29. It documents the conversation between a Muslim commander (*emir*) and a Christian monk, although the names of these two are not mentioned. On the question of global rule, the *emir* quotes the qur'anic verse from Surah *Al-Anbiya* (The Prophets), which is a literal quotation of Psalm 37:29: "and we have decreed in the book of Psalms (*zabūr*)—after admonition (*dhikr*)—that the righteous shall inherit the earth" (Q Al-Anbiya 21:105).

This verse is of paramount importance to the theology of salvation in the Qur'an and is reiterated in other qur'anic verses in which inheritance and righteousness are connected to one another. This conversation shows how the conquest of territories link to the favor of God and signify righteousness in early Islamic militancy. The evidence from the *Bet Hale Disputation* is of great significance because it is an independent witness to the centrality of Psalm 37:29 via Qur'an 21:105, and of how it was understood by early Muslims.

Al-Biqā'ī (aka Ibrāhīm ibn 'Umar Biqā'ī, 1406–1480) was the first Muslim exegete to inquire after the scriptural origins of the quotation in Qur'an 21:105. In the fifteenth century, al-Biqā'ī wrote a treatise called the "Just Verdict on the Permissibility of Quoting from the Ancient Scriptures." *Kitab al-Aqwāl al-qawīmah fī ḥukm al-naql min al-kutub al-qadīmah* is the most extensive discussion of the status of the Bible in Islam. At al-Azhar University in Cairo, al-Biqā'ī successfully defended his use of biblical references in his commentary on the Qur'an. The seminal work of al-Biqā'ī provides a foundation for using the Bible and the Qur'an for scriptural exposition in the cross-religious spectrum.

Emphasizing common ground between the Qur'an and the Bible is not a new idea. From the seventh through the fifteenth centuries, Muslim sources with biblical references are reliable although sporadic. Ibn Hazm, mentioned earlier, was a high scholar, jurist, and qur'anic elegist from Spain, and occupies a special status in Muslim history. He is among the earliest of his time to create scholarly comparative studies of the Bible and the Qur'an. Ibn Taymiyyah from Damascus, also mentioned earlier, also acquired an extensive knowledge of the contemporary scriptures of his age. Ibn Kammuna (d. 1284), a Jewish philosopher from Baghdad in the medieval era, was a biblical and qur'anic scholar whose treatise *Tanqih* (*Examination of the Three Faiths*) rejects the polemic nature of the dialogue between Muslim and Christian in regard to scriptural reasoning. Nevertheless, Christians and Muslims objected to the way he presented their tenets, and representatives of both religions wrote rebuttals.

Eastern Christian scholarship and theology developed within the Islamic context as a common cultural matrix to which both Christians and Muslims contributed, while remaining robustly Christian in content. Bayt al-Hikmah (House of Wisdom), a center for scholarship, was instituted to translate the Greek text of Scripture and other works into Arabic. The passing of the headship of Bayt al-Hikmah between Christian and Muslim scholars during the tenth century is a rare example of interaction between Christians and Muslims in that period. Jane Idleman Smith observes that Greek philosophy survived in the world of Islam not through the efforts of Muslim scholars, but through the work done by Arab and Assyrian Christians in translating the classics into Syriac and then into Arabic.[8]

Colonialism

Over time, militant crusades gave way to colonial influence and power plays, as slave, spice, and silk trade marked the beginning of the colonial era from the tenth century. Since Islam's inception in the early seventh century, all Eastern patriarchal sees, excluding Rome, came under Muslim rule for the next 1,400 years. This political and military success was considered a clear sign of God's favor for Muslim rulers. By 1500 CE, missionary efforts and imperialism tipped the balance of power away from the Islamic bloc to the Western monarchs.

The medieval era brought Portuguese missionaries to South Asia during the fifteenth century, and subsequently into the court of various Mughal emperors, including Akbar the Great. The Mughal Empire, a Muslim dynasty founded in 1526, ruled much of the Indian subcontinent for more than three hundred years. While medieval Europe lay under the shadow of inquisitions and the persecution of Christian heretics identified by the Roman Catholic Church, the Portuguese Jesuit priests were astonished to see Akbar's tolerance and interfaith harmony and his respect for other religions.

Jesuit missionaries presented to Akbar a copy of a Bible printed for King Philip I of Spain in 1579, written in Hebrew, Greek, Latin, and Chaldean. Akbar reportedly "handled the holy text with deepest respect, took off his turban, touched the volume to his head and then kissed it."[9] Sadly, however, he was never able to read the foreign languages.

The Portuguese Jesuits focused on the languages of Persian and Turkish spoken by the court members and rulers, while ignoring the popular vernacular of the people—the Hindustani/Urdu language. Even Sunday services and catechism took place in Portuguese. They thought Arabic was an Islamic language of revelation and sought to grant Portuguese the same dignity. By 1611, they realized their mistake, but it was too late: They had failed to connect with common people on the common ground of language.

Jumping ahead to the nineteenth century, the Western Protestant mission took the mantle and brought the gospel to the Punjab in North India. Nineteenth-century engagement of Islam by the West exposed the interests of international diplomacy and expansionism and was known as the "heyday" of mission and imperialism. Two notable missionaries—Henry Martyn (1781–1812) in India and William Henry Temple Gairdner (1873–1928) in Cairo—used culturally sensitive and artistic means to reach Muslims. In contrast to these creative models, however, others brought the baggage of an apologetic and polemical approach to Islam in South Asia.

Presbyterian mission work began in the northwest part of the Indian subcontinent at Ludhiana in 1834. The outlook of

Christianity was urban and elite, as both missionaries and converts were based in towns and cities. Their contacts with rural people originally remained minimal and brief. In the 1870s, however, a large-scale conversion movement began among a low-caste people group in rural Punjab, and by 1900 a similar movement emerged among another low-caste group in the neighboring provinces. In these cases, the conversion movements transformed the Christian community, and the Presbyterian portion of it, into a much larger, overwhelmingly illiterate, impoverished, rural Dalit community.[10]

Muslim-Christian polemical attacks have a deep-rooted history. From the seventh century onward, Muslim scholars have accused the Bible, particularly the Torah and the *Injil* (Gospels), of *tahrif*—literally, "distortion" or "falsification." The same debates also occur about translations of the Qur'an. On one hand, the Qur'an acknowledges Christians as *Ahl al-Kitab*, "The People of the Book." However, those books—*Torah*, *Zabur*, and *Injil*—play almost no role in Islamic piety. A significant reason for Muslims neglecting what are often called "the previous scriptures" seems to be the way the Qur'an expresses ambivalent attitudes toward them.

Islamic art, organic and voice-centric, has roots in "the Book." Yet the artistic spirituality of Islam is largely absent during this time of Muslim-Christian engagement. Today's cultural milieu, in contrast, offers a broad opportunity to use musical arts in creative peacemaking approaches capable of paving a path for ongoing collaborations.

Sufism

A later chapter will explore in more detail the range of divergent attitudes toward music and art that have arisen over the centuries among the Muslim community. For now, however, this brief overview of historical Muslim-Christian engagement must include reference to an important development in the history of Islam.

In the midst of a great debate in Islam about the legitimacy of music in canonical worship, a movement emerged in the eighth century called Sufism. Sufis give music and spiritual dance a prominent role in enabling Muslims to mystically enter into a closer relationship with God. The contemplative and spiritual nature of Sufi Islam is truly a crossroads for interfaith engagement toward harmony and extraordinary peacemaking within a cultural tradition. Sufi spirituality provides a gateway for Christians to develop relationships with the Muslim world.

Sufi shrines are established in all regions, and the one commonality in all these shrines is music. Apart from the cultural, ethnic, linguistic, geographical, political, theological, and sectarian divisions in the Islamic world, there is a bonding factor of religious musical culture that brings people together for spiritual nourishment and interfaith relationships in the Islamic context. We will look at the possibilities and opportunities for Muslim-Christian engagement through Sufism later in this book.

Hope for Fruitful Outcomes

As religious scholars pursue the parallels and common ground among the sacred scriptures of the monotheistic faith traditions, new paths are forming and building bridges to the world of Islam. The book of Psalms/Zabur plays a key role for these peacemaking processes as the sacred text gets translated into local languages and communicated through musical forms reflecting the cultural context.

In the twenty-first century, scholarly engagement with these interreligious scriptures continues, as seen in the work of Javed Ahmad Ghamidi (1951–). As a Muslim reformist and Qur'an exegetist, his nonviolent approach, based on comprehensive hermeneutical methods of Islamic jurisprudence, provides a convincing interpretation in support of coexistence between non-Muslims and different sects of Islam. He publicly opposes the blasphemy laws in Pakistan and convinces readers that the Sermon on the Mount by Jesus Christ in Matthew 5–7 is the constitution of God's kingdom for the Muslim community as well. His conclusions have challenged the religious status quo and resulted in his currently living in Dallas, Texas due to violent atrocities perpetrated against his work and companions.

I believe the first two waves of Christianity in what is now Pakistan—the first-century St. Thomas in Taxila and the sixteenth-century Portuguese mission to the Mughal court—died out in part due to their lack of utilizing the vernacular and contextual musical resources. Thankfully, mission-minded believers have begun taking a different approach over the last hundred-plus years. Recognizing the common heritage of the book of Psalms/Zabur for both Christianity and Islam, as well as its capacity to address both of these deficiencies, gives us hope for much more fruitful outcomes from engagement between the two faiths. Now, more than ever, this shared resource is opening doors for building Muslim-Christian friendships of understanding and peace in the twenty-first century.

Notes

1 Alan P. Merriam, *The Anthropology of Music* (Evanston, IL: Northwestern University Press, 1964), 32.

2 Christopher Small, *Musicking: The Meanings of Performing and Listening* (Middletown, CT: Wesleyan University Press, 1998), 9.

3 Roberta R. King and Sooi Ling Tan, "From Beirut to Yogyakarta," in *(Un)common Sounds: Songs of Peace and Reconciliation among Muslims and Christians*, eds. Roberta R. King and Sooi Ling Tan (Eugene, OR: Cascade Books, 2014), 6, 12–13.

4 Sheema Kermani, personal interview with the author February 19, 2019, in Karachi, Pakistan.

5 See Muhammad Ibn 'Abd Allah, *Six Covenants of the Prophet Muhammad with the Christians of His Time: The Primary Documents*, ed. Andrew John Morrow (Tacoma, WA: Covenants Press, 2015).

6 Martin Lings, *Muhammad: His Life Based on the Earliest Sources* (United Kingdom: Inner Traditions International, 1983), 300.

7 A. Mingana, *Timothy's Apology for Christianity* (Cambridge: W. Heffer & Sons Ltd., 1928), http://www.tertullian.org/fathers/timothy_i_apology_00_intro.htm

8 Jane Idleman Smith, *Muslims, Christians, and the Challenge of Interfaith Dialogue* (Oxford, UK: Oxford University Press, 2007), 35.

9 Annemarie Schimmel, *The Empire of the Great Mughals: History, Art and Culture*, ed. Burzine K Waghmar, trans. Corinne Atwood (London: Reaktion Books, 2004), 120.

10 See John C. B. Webster, *A Social History of Christianity: North-West India Since 1800* (New Delhi: Oxford University Press, 2007).

Performance
Bandish

3

Sur-Sangam
Musical Heritage of Pakistan

In chapter 1, I defined the term *sur-sangam*, a compound word from *sur* (musical note) and *sangam*, the Sanskrit word for confluence. For our purposes, it is a broadly useful term describing a meeting place or blend of text and tune, souls and minds, ethnomusicology and anthropology, qur'anic and biblical streams.

In Pakistan, any attempt to build a musical bridge to connect people from Muslim and Christian faith traditions must rely on the primary building block of the raga. The raga, also defined in chapter 1, is the melodic basis of the classical music of the Indian subcontinent.

Ragas are historical systems of music. The raga resembles a scale in a Western musical system but is also a "meaning system." A raga is composed of *surs* (notes or keys on a piano) in a particular scale. Using the image of pottery, ragas are like a clay (raw material) from the subcontinent's soil to be made into a pot on the potter's wheel of the composer's imagination.

The raga is a set of notes expressing human emotions. The primary significance of ragas is their ability to affect and attract human emotional intensity and spirituality. For this reason, using the raga as the musical foundation for interfaith outreach among Indo-Pakistani cultures will naturally open doors and hearts, yielding fruitful dialogue.

Before we can blend text and tune for culturally relevant communication of the Good News, it is essential to understand the Indic music system of raga or *raag*, redeemed from Hindu mythology by the text of the book of Psalms.

Indic Music System of Raga

A raga should be no fewer than five notes. There are three kinds of ragas: pentatonic (*arruv*), hexatonic (*kharruv*), and heptatonic (*sampooran*). A raga could be described by its characteristics of *arohi* and *amrohi*—an ascending and descending pattern of *sargam*, a set of seven notes: *Sa, Re, Ga, Ma, Pa, Dha, Ni* (compare to Do, Re, Mi, Fa, So, La, Ti of Western scales). Five of these seven notes further divide into four *surtis* (small microtonal units) for a total of twenty-two *surtis* in the octave.[1] Each raga contains four structural characteristics of *surti*, *sur*, *vadi*, and *samvadi*. The moveable Sa (*kharaj*) is equal to the tonic of the major scale that can be adjusted or in tune according to the preferred pitch of singers or congregation.

The first written treatise on the Indian classical music of ragas and rhythms was compiled by the Indian musicologist Vishnu Narayan Bhatkhande (1860–1936).[2] Ragas are classified by a variety of criteria. Here are a few categories: number of notes, time of day, the personification of the principal raga (six raga*s* are considered male, thirty-six *raginis* female), the *thaat* system (framework for arranging the seven notes of the scale; Bhatkhande's system has ten *thaats*), and *rasa* (emotions).[3]

The figure 1.1 illustrates the complex circle of raga classification.

Classification of Raga, *Rasa*, and *Taal*

During the ninth century, there was a bewildering musical classification system in the Indian subcontinent. Music *gurus* (teachers) introduced the concept of raga and *ragini* (male and female) from the

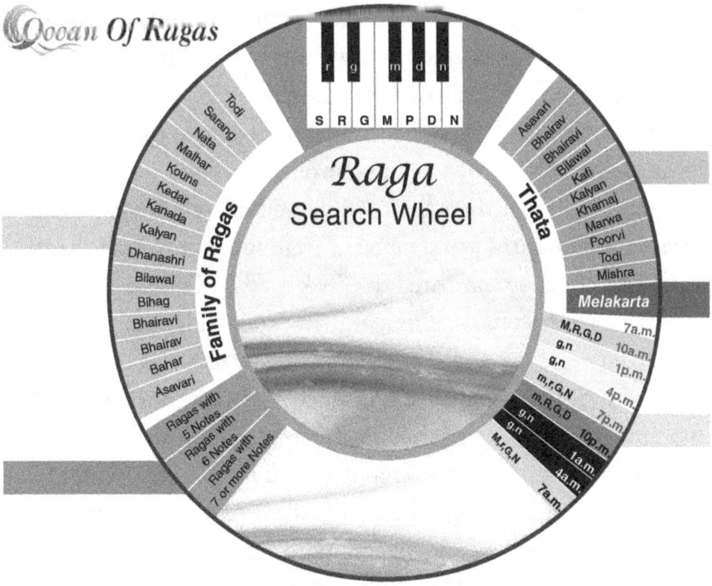

Figure 1.1. Raga classification. Source: Scarlet India, Ocean of Ragas http://oceanofragas.com/Raga_search_wheel.aspx.

fourteenth through the nineteenth centuries. This system consisted of six male patriarchal ragas, each having five or six *raginis* (wives) as well as sons (*putra*) and daughters-in-law. This classification also represented the relational and communal culture of South West Asia. Ragas are described in terms of the personification of family and community. The third classification was introduced again on the basis of scales, and this classification was adopted by Bhatkhande. His work was known as the most influential and pragmatic raga classification, and was based on ten heptatonic scale types called *thaat* (framework). According to Bhatkhande's system, "the *thaat* is a scale using all seven notes including Sa (first note) and Pa (fifth note). In his system, all ragas are grouped under ten scale types, each of which is named after a prominent raga that uses the note verities in question."[4]

Ragas are used for daily Hindu worship in temples and homes and for names of Hindu deities. The oral traditional music of India is related to the universe's harmony, in contrast to the structured tonal music of Western tradition. Systems of *thaat* for ragas are classified according to such categories as season, feeling, and mood of human nature. They are also classified according to the time of day. For instance, *bhairav thaat* (early morning raga) is more contemplative and devotional than the friendly and cheerful *ragini bhairavi* (daytime *ragini*) or the joyful mood of evening *bilawal thaat* in a major scale. This could be compared to Greek modes of music like Dorian or Phrygian that were also thought to have particular characteristics.

Two more ways to classify ragas are by *rasa* and *taal*:

Rasa (literally "juice" or "essence"): Indian music is divided into nine emotional categories. Each category represents a different human emotion. Ragas are characterized by the quasi-emotional affects in the *rasas* of love, heroism, disgust, anger, mirth, terror, compassion, wonder, and peace, with some systems adding a tenth *rasa* of devotion. Music composers select a raga according to the text and compose a tune with a *rasa* reflecting the emotional requirement of the text or occasion.

Taal (rhythm patterns): A famous musical proverb says, "A person without melodic understanding or *sur* (musical note) can sing, but without rhythmic understanding can't sing." *Taal* refers to *tali* (clap). The circle of *taal* starts and ends at the first *tali*. The completion of the circle is called *sam* (a foot of a horse). Usually *taal* is accompanied by the *tabla,* small two-piece hand drums covered with the stretched skin of a cow or goat, and *dholak* (a cylinder-style drum instrument). The Indian rhythm is complex, and a player uses an additive rhythm in regular, double, triple, and quadruple times. The Indian rhythm and metric cycle are classified in 120 *taals*. The most common *taals* are eight-beat *kehrwa* and six-beat *dadra*. Both rhythms are used in musical compositions of the Punjabi Zabur/Psalms.[5] The sound of Indian drums and rhythm patterns are known for their cheerful and heart-rending emotional effects. The combinations of *taal* and raga (rhythmic and melodic utterances) communicate emotional expressions.

Relevant or Compromised?

A prevailing controversy continues to smolder in Pakistani–Christian communities about using ragas as a worship style. During the singing of psalms or hymns, gospel singers usually get criticized for using ragas and *sargam* (the pattern of seven musical notes), because the names of these notes are associated with Hindu mythology.

This is a universal struggle in every culture. Contemporary Western worship leaders who are compared to rock stars face similar challenges.[6] Martin Luther was criticized for using secular tunes with spiritual words, and John Calvin used the same familiar music from everyday common life in the Reformed Genevan church. C. Randall Bradley asserts, "Christ came to redeem the world, and Christ can redeem any music."[7] This is true for ragas on the South-Asian subcontinent as well.

Through the work of the Holy Spirit, the sacred text of the book of Psalms has redeemed these ragas from Hindu mythology to be associated with the Word of God and integrated them as part of congregational singing. Using cultural tunes embedded with the words of Scripture allows musicians and singers to worship and praise God by using their authentic South-Asian heritage in their heart music and heart language. And the *sur-sangam* convergence of these same cultural tunes with psalm texts in the vernacular provides a platform to promote peace-making and Muslim-Christian friendship in the twenty-first century.

Pakistani Music Genres: Folk Music

During my doctoral dissertation research, I asked a group of singers and scholars what they perceived as the music genres in Pakistan. Their responses were classified into five significant categories: folk music, classical music, religious songs, Sufi music, and film or popular music. My research focused on only the first four genres, relevant to my topic.

In addition to the raga-based classical music previously discussed, folk music is the communal and cultural expression of the common people of Pakistan. It is the most popular and historical oral tradition in the country. According to one of the singers I interviewed, regional folk music is actually the origin of classical music. "Folk [music] births classical music," affirmed Murtaza Khan Niazi, a Muslim music teacher who belongs to a Pashtun tribal people group and is head of the music academy in Karachi. Then in turn, "classical music could serve as an anchor or base ground for music culture." He further explained that "classical music became an academic and educational discipline with rules and science of practice and performance, while folk [music] kept its original form."[8]

Pakistan has more than seventy-five ethnic linguistic groups, and each ethnic group has its musical tradition. The folk music in Pakistan can be categorized by regions, such as Baluchi, Punjabi, Potohari, Sindhi, Kashmiri, Saraiki, Pashto, and Hindko music.[9] However, due to the historical and cultural development of music, published Sufi poetic literature, and government support, the Punjab and Sindh provinces of Pakistan have played a particularly influential role in the music culture of Pakistan. Folk songs reflect various occasions—marriage, birth, death, harvest festivals, village fairs, and courtship. Musicianship as an occupation is passed through heredity. Folk singers sing stories and transmit their heritage to their children to keep the legacy of folk singing. The majority of musicians belong to the lower classes. The music features instruments typical to the subcontinent, such as the sitar, harmonium, tabla and dholak drums, and the bansuri, a type of flute.

In sum, it is said that the primary significance of ragas is their ability to affect and attract human emotional intensity and spirituality. The folk and classical music of the Indian subcontinent finds its roots in the socioreligious context of cultural history and tradition, and expresses cognitive and emotive behavior. A fuller understanding of the dimension of historic Indic musicality will incorporate the concept of *sangeet*: the totality of vocalization, instrument playing, and dancing. The whole music system is based on relational, hierarchical, and geographical backgrounds that further divide into various genres. Three things are critical in this tradition: *gharana*, *guru*, and *genre* (family, teacher, and form of music, respectively). The authenticity of a teacher comes from their musical *gharana*. The hereditary system of *gharanas* (literally "families") refers to modes and styles of both singing and instrument playing.

Ordinary people sing and practice folk music in their everyday life, while classical music has become a professional occupation. The classification of music genres, the hierarchy of *gharanas*, and the oral tradition of transmitting music education show that music as a cultural text is historically rooted in the soil. The breadth and width of the musical spectrum of Pakistan are vast, and music is in the DNA of the culture, which runs in the blood and bones of the nation.

Religious Music: Canonical, Noncanonical, and Sufi

As a music genre, religious music takes the issue of music culture to a deeper level. Concerning the status of music in Islam, four things need to be considered: vocal art and the distinction between recitation and song, the terminology of music, instrumental performance, and the issue of halal and haram (that which is permitted or prohibited). The next chapter will explore these issues in more depth.

For now, we will simply outline the three main categories in the realm of religious music in Pakistan: canonical, noncanonical, and Sufi music. Religion engulfs every fiber of the society, including music. Every religious tradition in the Indian subcontinent speaks the same musical language and fetches their songs from one of these three streams.

The lawful or canonical practice of music in Islam relates to two sacred vocal arts: the *qirat* (recitation of the Qur'an) and the *Adhan* (call to prayer). Both practices are done only in the Arabic language and based on the voice-centric science of *tajwīd*. The *tajwīd* is a vocal technique of cantillation and permitted embellishments that constitutes the only compulsory *masjid* (mosque) music in Muslim culture. Cantillation is not considered melodic music, even though it is pitched. The recitation of the Qur'an, therefore, has become the primary example of pitched sound-art in the Islamic world.

Noncanonical religious or spiritual music takes place outside the *masjid* (mosque)—vocal art in social spaces. It is cultural and contextual, based in the native vernacular language. This religious music uses raga- and *taal*-based melodic and rhythmic structures for singing. Optional hymns are meant to enhance festive occasions, in particular, celebrations such as Ramadan nights, Muhammad's birthday (*mawlid*) and death anniversaries, the birthdays or death anniversaries of Sufi imams (*urs*), weddings, and funeral condolences.

The third main category of religious music in Pakistan is Sufi music. Sufism is a "parallel religion" to canonical or doctrinal Islàm in Muslim societies. Shrine-based Sufi music includes both folk and classical styles, and adds the artistic expression of dance, instruments, and singing. My research has revealed significant opportunities within the Sufi movement to build bridges of peace between Muslims and Christians, and we will explore this potential in more detail.

A Vibrant Music Culture

We have found that the music culture of Pakistan is rich and vibrant. Pakistan is an oral culture, and music serves as a tool for communication and cultural cohesion. Every member of the society uses the same musical language and sources to produce and consume music, whether sacred or secular. Voice remains the predominant genre for musical performance. Whether music is used for religious or familiar purposes, it grips the human heart with honesty. Christopher Small's theoretical framework of musicking describes music as a binding and connecting force for the participants involved in the whole process.

On the grassroots level, the common people use music in religious and ritualistic practices. Whether responding to a natural tragedy or terrorism or a matter of pride, the whole nation unites through songs. The Pakistani army releases a music video after every tragedy and uplifts the morale of the nation.[10] The Taliban themselves endorse songs that legitimize their ideology,[11] and extremists use religious poetry and songs to recruit, inspire, and motivate *jihadis* (holy warriors) and *mujahidin* (militants). Missiology needs to address the challenge of this Islamic musical approach and provide a counter-narrative as an antidote. Art can help to break the misconceptions of Islamophobia and resolve the Western myth of the religious Other, including our Muslim neighbors. The concept of music culture and musicking have capacity to foster Muslim-Christian friendship based on the principle of *sur-sangam* confluence.

Notes

1 I-to Loh, *Hymnal Companion to Sound the Bamboo: Asian Hymns in Their Cultural and Liturgical Context* (Chicago: GIA Publications, Inc., 2011), 21. These twenty-two *surtis* come from microtones of five notes: Re, Ga, Ma, Dha, Ni; each of these notes divides into four *surtis*, 5×4=20. Sa and Pa stand for a single note and do not contain any additional *surti*. Thus 20+2=22 *surtis*.

2 Janaki Bakhle, *Two Men and Music: Nationalism and the Making of an Indian Classical Tradition* (Oxford: Oxford University Press, 2005), https://youtu.be/VoCA13WxQ4c

3 Bakhle, *Two Men and Music;* https://www.parampara-sg.org/single-post/2016/01/02/Classification-of-Raga

4 Joep Bor, ed., *The Raga Guide: A Survey of 74 Hindustani Ragas* (London: Zenith Media for Nimbus Records with Rotterdam Conservatory of Music, 1999), 3.

5 The notation and sound of *dadra* on the *tabla* is [dhin dhin na dha tou na]. It is a six-beat circular rhythm with one clap on the first beat of every circle. *Kehrwa* has eight beats with various styles and patterns. The most common sounds are [dha gay na ti ta key na ti], and [dhi dhi ka ta na kay dhi na].

6 Daniel Darling, *Friday Five: Stephen Miller*, 2013, https://www.christianitytoday.com/pastors/2013/august-online-only/friday-five-stephen-miller.html

7 C. Randall Bradley, *From Memory to Imagination: Reforming the Church's Music* (Grand Rapids, MI: William B. Eerdmans Publishing Company, 2012), 109.

8 Murtaza Khan Niazi, personal interview with the author March 17, 2019, in Karachi, Pakistan.

9 See Sain Zahoor, "Allah Allah Bol O Bndy," performed 2017, https://youtu.be/STgrwlUvKH8 and https://folkcloud.com/song/422/sain-zahoor/allah-allah-bol-o-bndy

10 See, for example, https://www.youtube.com/watch?v=yoLEomk-V38.

11 "Taliban Has Come" is a song in praise of the Taliban in Pakistan: https://www.youtube.com/watch?v=siUHzt9TIlw.

4

Islamic Views of Art and Music

Concerning the role of musical art in Islam, Muslim thought looks back to the sixth century and to the life of the Prophet of Islam, as it does for every social and religious practice. The actions and sayings of Muhammad are considered the perfect role model for Muslim society everywhere. Every Muslim strives to live and follow the *Sīra* (life) and *sunnah* (actions) of the Prophet.

Thus Islamic thought is based on two primary sources: the Qur'an as divine revelation and the Hadith as the record of the sayings and actions of Muhammad. (The Hadith is often considered together with *Sīra*, prophetic biography.) What emerged from my research analysis relates to the poetic nature of the Qur'an and its relationship to vocal recitation. In oral tradition, voice is a tool for communication and education.

Although music is such a vital part of oral Arabic culture, the Qur'an is surprisingly silent about music. Nevertheless, the book of Psalms has found various convergences with the Qur'an. These will be discussed in detail in the next chapter. It is the Hadith tradition that provides the bulk of quotations in Islam against or in support of music.

In Islam and the Arab world, "music" has been defined almost exclusively as vocal art, designated by the Arabic word *ghina* (song). In the Indian subcontinent, terms such as *gana* or *ghina* in Arabic denote singing in Hindu/Urdu, and connote lightness and frivolity, if not debauchery. "Singing" and "music" (*musiqi*) are considered definitely unfit for Muslims praying in a *masjid* (mosque). In the context of the mosque, the *ulama* (religious scholars) use different verbs such as *parhna* in Urdu, which means primarily "to read or recite," when referring to the pitched sound art of cantillation.

Ghina (Singing)

"*Ghina* is a greater sin." This quotation, in black spray paint, is written among various others on the white background of the mosque walls facing toward the main university road in Karachi. This statement shows the vagueness in the usage of the term "music." Use of the term "music" is one of the perplexing issues in the Islamic world; one which has continued over the centuries and needs clarification.

Ghina describes melodic recitations that are musically equivalent to singing but conceptually distinct from music. Classical dance teacher Sheema Kermani, one of my interviewees, grieves that "In Pakistan, we put art away, we look down on it, we look [at it as] immoral, we say that they are against our religion."[1] This form of terminological distinction extends also to the persons who perform, so vocalists are called *gawaiya*, or singers of a particular genre.

For this same reason, religious singers are distinct from commercial singers. They have their own titles to differentiate them from contemporary commercial singing. The Islamic religious singers—*a cappella* (unaccompanied) voice-centric singers—have unique titles and are celebrated by their respective religious sects. For instance, qur'anic reciters are *qaris*. *Muezzin* is a person who calls for prayer. The Sunni religious singers are *naat-khwan* or *humd-khwan*, a Shi'a reciter is *azadar*, and Sufi singers are *qawwal.*

Parhna (Reciting)

The verb *parhna* in Urdu means primarily "to read or recite," and stands in contrast to singing. Melodic recitations may be musically equivalent to singing but conceptually different from music. Even when classical ragas are employed during such recitations, they nevertheless are considered distinct from the realm of singing.

Undoubtedly, the human voice is a crown of Islamic religious art. Vocal music was chief of art, song, and poetry during the Prophet's day and stayed in honor after his lifetime. Vocal art is the most revered and accepted for Islamic religious purposes. Instruments, in contrast, are culturally restricted, while using voice with any embellishment has no restrictions. My interviewees confirmed that the most important thing for recitation is a good voice.

The terminology and words used in and for religious music have an impact on social behavior. Unaccompanied vocal art in recitation of sacred scripture is acceptable and revered in the Islamic music culture.

Pre-Islamic Art

Although in Muslim hagiography the pre-Islamic period in Arabia was perceived as *djahiliyya* (barbaric and backward), the Arabs of that era were proud of their epic tales, heart-rending poetry, and eloquent prose. In seventh-century Arabia, poetry was the chief art and was recited orally in public contests at Ukaz, near Mecca. The winner's poetic piece was called the *Mu'allagat* (suspended) as it was customary to hang outstanding examples of the genre in the Ka'aba, the Meccan shrine. Ancient Arabs believed that the poet (*sha'ir*, *shu'ara* pl.) and the musician had special relationships with the spirits (*djinn*) and acquired supernatural powers from them. Skillful poets epitomized classical poetry with rhythm and rhymes, and enhanced it by chanting it in public recitation.

The issue of the poetic authenticity of the Qur'an is so important that the twenty-sixth surah (chapter) of the Qur'an is entitled Surah *Al-Shu'ara*, or "The Poets." The qur'anic revelation of the prophet Muhammad was considered a challenge to the genius of Arab poets, and the ensuing conflict was recorded in Qur'an Al Shuara 26:224–27, where the prophet Muhammad was accused of poetic forgery. Scholars assert that Muhammad was not acquainted with the poetic arts, whereas the Meccans were armed with one of their most potent weapons—poetry—against him.

The antagonism between the Prophet and the poets in Mecca became so furious that when Muhammad gained power in Medina, he commanded the assassination of various male and female poets. Moreover, the Prophet also employed other poets to counter his enemies, but apparently his enemies did not have the power to kill or to expel Muhammad or his poets.

Apart from violent raids and assassinations of the poets, Medina hosted a vibrant artistic Arab community. Arab vocal and musical arts were influenced by Persian and Sassanian culture. During the time of Muhammad, Islamic songs were nonexistent, and all artistic energies were instead on one favorite theme—love. This love poetry, set to appropriate melodies, had roots in the pre-Islamic *qasida*, a laudatory, elegiac, or satiric Arabic poem, often telling a story such as the desert adventures of a wayward mistress hunting the onager.

Early Muslim historians describe pre-Islamic music as the simple folk songs heard in the Bedouin tribal music encampments. The oldest type is the *huda*, a simple song and the first song genre.

Simple genres include those sung during the watering of animals, a practice that reflects the importance of water in a dry area.

The arrival of Islam did not change at all the attraction exercised by vocal music, song, and poetry—these were honored during the lifetime of the Prophet as well as after. Muhammad transmitted the revelation to his followers through the prevailing method of oral tradition.

Muhammad's Experience

According to the Islamic sources, the Qur'an is the revealed word of Allah (God) to the prophet Muhammad over a period of twenty years in the early decades of the sixth century CE. It was "laid upon the heart" of Muhammad when subsequently rehearsed with the angel Gabriel.[2] The Qur'an is considered as the "sound of a divine utterance, the sound of God," and the generating source has ultimate authority within Islam.

Muhammad's mystical experience is recorded in the Qur'an in Surah 17 *Al-Isra'* ("The Night Journey"/"Children of Israel") and also in Hadith tradition. According to these accounts, in addition to his mystical state during his time of solitude and encounter with the angel Gabriel in the cave of Hira, Muhammad underwent a mystical odyssey to seventh heaven *(al-'Isrā' wal-Mi'rāj)* in the two parts of a Night Journey that he took during a single night around the year 621 CE. It has been described as both a physical and spiritual journey.

From the mystical experience of the Prophet, the sound of music, apparently, was a main element through which he received revelation. He reportedly told followers he sometimes heard a "knell of bell" prior to a revelation, and this sound had a strong effect on him. This detail calls to mind a possible connection with the bells on the hem of the high priest's robe in Israel's wilderness tabernacle (Exodus 28:33, 39:25–26).

Muhammad's attitude toward art was positive and he was inclined to the existing art of the pre-Islamic Arab peninsula. Moreover, the Qur'an is silent on sanctioning any musical practice for religious purposes, providing space for artistic expression in Islam.

Qirat: Recitation of the Qur'an

The qur'anic command and Hadith traditions allow the practice of *qirat*—recitation of the Qur'an. The history of the qur'anic revelation illustrates the relevance of the statement that the scripture was brought to humans "in a clear, Arabic tongue" (Q Al-Shaura 26:195). The divine message had to be proclaimed clearly. "Recite the Qur'an very distinctively!" was the command given to Muhammad (Q Al-Muzzammil 73:4). The Prophet, in a hadith, recommended to the faithful, "Beautify the Qur'an with your voices. Verily, a beautiful voice adds to the beauty of the Qur'an" (Sunan Abī Dāwūd 1468).

Islamic tradition considers secular music spiritually suspect. Hence, recitation of the Qur'an, even if it sounds musical, is not conceived of as music. Many Muslims do not consider the qur'anic recitation to be a musical activity, but mostly neutral and value-free art. At the same time, *qaris* (Qur'an reciters) use various styles of recitation, called *tilawat*, and distinctive forms of *tajwīd* (embellishment of recitation) to give their vocal art appealing melodies and intonations.

Ethnomusicologist Michael Frishkopf makes the following insightful observation:

> The terminological distinctions among different forms of vocal practice must be carefully heeded. Islam has historically adopted a restricted view toward the use of music as a means of religious expression; the

terms used both reveal and protect the conceptual boundaries constructed to surround various kinds of vocalization, all of which would naïvely be labeled "singing" or "music" by the English-speaking non-culture bearer.[3]

Adhan: A Dream of the Devotees

Every Muslim is commanded to perform ritual prayer (*salat-namaz*) five times a day. The five prayer times are *Fajr* (pre-dawn), *Zuhr* (noon), *Asr* (afternoon), *Maghrib* (sunset), and *Isha* (evening). The reminder to pray comes via the *Adhan*, a call to prayer from the minaret of the *masjid* (mosque). From this tower balcony, the *muezzin* (reciter) summons Muslims five times a day for obligatory devotion. *Adhan* is both a proclamation and an invitation to the oneness of God (*tauheed*).

Adhan was instituted by the prophet Muhammad between 622 and 624 CE in Medina. The first *muezzin* was an Abyssinian *mawla* (slave) named Bilal ibn Rabah (d. 641).

Adhan starts by the proclamation of the *takbir* ("God is greatest") and the *kalima* (creed: "I bear witness ..."). Here is the text of *Adhan*:

Allah u Akbar — God is The Greatest (4 times)
Ash-hadu alla ilaha illallah — I bear witness that there is no lord except God (2 times)
Ash-hadu anna Muhammadan rasulullah — I bear witness that Muhammad is the Messenger of God (2 times)
Hayya' alas-salat — Make haste toward prayer (2 times)
Hayya' alal-falah — Make haste toward welfare [success] (2 times)
Allah u Akbar — God is The Greatest (2 times)
La ilaha illallah — There is no lord except God (1 time)

According to Islamic history, the tradition of *Adhan* started from Medina. It is interesting to note that the Islamic creed was not written in the Qur'an in its actual revealed text, nor was it initiated by the Prophet. It has derived from a historical incident. The call to prayer came through a simultaneous dream of a few followers (*sahaba*) of Muhammad, and was endorsed and accepted by the Prophet. Describing the history of *Adhan*, an imam of the Karachi grand mosque, Abdullah Memmon, states, "When the Muslim population was increasing in Medina, the challenge was how to inform people about the time of prayer. There was not any regularized method at that time," and they wanted to differentiate from the Jewish practice of *shofar* (Arabic *naqoor*) as a call of prayer.

> The various followers came to the Prophet and shared their dream from last night. In their dream, they heard someone reciting these words of *Adhan*. In the morning, one follower came to the Prophet and shared these words of *Adhan*. Meanwhile, another came and shared the same dream. So, a couple of followers had the same dream about *Adhan*. Then the Prophet said to them, "Go and ask Bilal to repeat and recite those words and then he may use these for the call of every prayer." Since then, these words are used for *Adhan*.[4]

Thus, while the text of *Adhan* is not taken from the Qur'an, the concepts are derived from it. "The Prophet heard, he authenticated, and permitted to use it," Memmon said. He also affirmed that "these words are not written in the Qur'an. It is Allah's gift through the dreams of the followers. Then the prophet Muhammad authorized to initiate the call of prayer. [Later] it became the command and law."[5]

The Tune of *Adhan*

As previously mentioned, the first *muezzin* was not an Arab, but an Ethiopian slave. The tune was also set by the same African slave Bilal, living in Medina. Concerning the tune of *Adhan*, Imam Memmon said that "whatever style and sound he [Bilal] uttered, the Prophet permitted." At the conquest of Mecca, Muhammad "called Bilal and asked him to go to the rooftop of the *Bait-Allah-Ka'aba* [black cube at the shrine in Mecca] and recite *Adhan*."[6] In his lifetime, the Prophet always asked Bilal to recite *Adhan*. After the Prophet's death, Bilal migrated to some other place, and then other local people did the job.

Artistically, *Adhan* is considered as *tilawat* (sacred recitation) in the Arabic poetic genre. Moreover, the style of *Adhan* is flexible. There are five melodic variables in each call of prayer. *Adhan* has also passed through various changes, including an addition to the dawn prayer call. (The addition is a Hadith tradition: "Prayer is better than sleep," recited twice, usually inserted after "Make haste towards welfare.") *Adhan* is a domain of melodic creativity. Moreover, the oral tradition of transmitting knowledge and skills is the same as what professional musicians do in their own traditional and hierarchical domain. The sound of *Adhan* ranges from pure intonation to elaborated melody, depending on the vocal ability and training of the *muezzin*. In contrast with the sound of church bells or the Jewish shofar, *Adhan* is verbal and explicit. While *Adhan* is being recited from the *masjid*, everybody notices and offers respect for the moment: women cover their heads, and men join the congregation. Many Muslim musicians cease to play music during *Adhan*.

Tajwīd: Embellishment of Recitation

The musical aspects of the recitation of the Qur'an in Arabic developed from the melodies and intonations of the Arabs. We have noted the distinction Islam makes between song and cantillation, in which the rhythm and any embellishments to the recited text are subordinate to the textual content. The recitation (*qirat*) of the Qur'an is explicitly different from collective singing. It is directly linked to the vocal and sound art techniques that stimulate emotional affects on the listeners, and the ability of a reciter to "make people weep" (cf. Q Mariam 19:58; Al-Maidah 5:83), for weeping is a response to the truth. In the same manner that *Adhan* uses different modes of cantillation, *qirat* also can vary according to region, but the same homogeneous structure appears in all these modes.

During the early centuries of Islam, a detailed system developed concerning the rules of allowable *tajwīd* (embellishment of recitation). The directives sought to preserve the divine sound of the revelation and guard it against distortion. An important part of embellishment is the pause between phrases. The pause, one of the significant attributes of the cantillation, was likely inspired by classical patterns of rhythm and sound used in poetry.

Imam Abdullah Memmon expanded on the difference between singing and recitation of the Qur'an:

> There are restrictions in our *tajwīd* system. If a person stays in these restrictions, then it will not be *tajwīd* singing. However, if anyone crosses those restrictions, then it will change to a singing style. Our Prophet barred us from singing in the law. Prophet said about both *Adhan* and *qirat*: concerning *qirat* he said, "adopt the accent of Arab and avoid the *Ajam*" [Persian/non-Arabic]. Do not sound with rounding tongues. Make it simple as it is in singing. So, there is a difference between *qirat* and singing.[7]

Noncanonical Religious Music

In contrast to the sacred canonical practice of *qirat* and *Adhan* from the mosque, noncanonical religious music features vocal art in social spaces. This music, using local and regional cultural forms and vernacular languages, evolved to a position as art during social and religious events. Sunni, Shi'a, and Sufi streams of Islam all contribute to the religious music culture in Pakistan. Genres of noncanonical religious music include *naat*, *hamd*, *rajzia*, *manqabat*, and *marsiya*, among others.

The Sunni Stream

Naat is lyrical poetry in praise of the Islamic prophet Muhammad. In particular, the subject of the Prophet's birth has given rise to a great wealth of literary compositions and devotional songs. In contrast to the Arabic origin of the qur'anic recitation and the *Adhan*, *naat* is contextual in Islamic cultures. Many of the famous scholars in the earlier days of Islam wrote *naat*. *Naat* reciters are known as *naat-khwan* or *sana-khwan*. The practice is popular in South Asia, including Pakistan, India, and Bangladesh. Devotional hymns sung in Urdu or Punjabi typically use melodies composed in raga-based music. *Naat* is sung and written in local and regional languages and music styles.

In Pakistan, the subjects and themes of *naat* are two-fold: praising Prophet (*midhat-e-Rasool*) and love of Prophet (*ishq-e-Rasool*). Based on these two concepts, various radical religious groups use the slogan of "Ishq-e-Rasool" as an excuse to attack or kill anyone accused of blasphemy. The B and C clauses of Pakistan's blasphemy law are based on this same understanding of the "love of Prophet" concept. "That is why any blasphemy against the Prophet is unacceptable to Muslims. Even in the Prophet's own time, whoever disrespects him, he was assassinated"—so commented one scholar I interviewed.[8]

Hamd is poetry in praise of Allah (distinct from praise of the Prophet). It takes similar forms to *naat*. Another genre, *rajzia*, refers to songs sung during Islamic wars, for battle passion. An earlier pre-Islamic category of *rajzia* was patriotic poetry. *Manqabat* is sung in praise of Awliayh (saints), Hazrat Ali, and Imam Husain, as Sufi leaders.

The Shi'a Stream

The Muslim world is divided into two mainstream sects. The majority is Sunni or "orthodox" Muslim; the other sect is the community of the Shi'a or *fiqh Jafferia*. Shi'ites organize *majlis-e-soz* and *noha-matam* (gatherings of mourning, sorrow, and chest-beating, either gently striking the hand on the chest or vigorous forms of self-mortification) and *sham-e-ghariban* (an evening of vulnerable grievers) during the month of Muharram al-haram, the first month of the Islamic calendar, in which they commemorate the massacre of Muhammad's family in Karbala. The Karbala tragedy happened in 680 CE (61 AH of the Islamic calendar), when the Umayyad caliph Yazid (a traditional rival of the Prophet's tribe, from Banu Umayyad) killed Husain (grandson of the Prophet from Banu Hashim tribe) and many other male members of his family over the issue of the seat and title of the caliphate. This event birthed the Shi'a movement.

These gatherings for congregational grief, lament, and remembrance constitute a depository of Shi'a heritage, elucidation, and emotion and are structured with affective arrangement. Crying in the gathering is a sign of the ritual efficacy, and participants judge sermons and recitations accordingly. The emotive performance acts as music, recitation, and sermon, with visible kinds of bodily practices.

Marsiya (literally "mourning" or "lamentation") and *noha* are practices of grief with song. Distinct hymns that prompt all spiritual and emotional aspects of mourning, commitment, and commemoration are combined in a structure that takes the participants from tunes conveying introspective personal grief (*soz*) through dramatic narrative poetry (*marsiya*) and an oration about the events of the Battle of Karbala, the demise of the slain, and the suffering of the survivors. Participants wear black dresses, sit on the floor, sob silently, and weep loudly during sermons while hearing the heart-wrenching voices of those leading the mourning, expressing the emotions of ardent anguish.[9] Poetry, chanting, and cantillation help Shi'a Muslims to express their intense devotional mourning.

Noticeably, all the Muslim artists interviewed during my doctoral research and those who sing gospel songs belong to Shi'a Muslim faith traditions. Shi'a Muslims in the Indian subcontinent developed the poetic genre of *marsiya* and *noha*. It is regarded as an act of piety and religious duty to eulogize and lament the martyrs of Karbala. The passionate poetry of this genre is composed in the highly emotive raga scales and chanted by the group in antiphonal style, accompanied by the chest-beating sound and rhythm. Musical instruments are not allowed. The practice of *marsiya* and *noha* singing has produced the majority of Muslim singers and musicians from the Shi'a faith traditions in Pakistan.

The Sufi Stream

Amid the great debate in Islam about the appropriateness of music in corporate worship, a movement was birthed early in the eighth century called Sufism. In this mystical tradition, music has played a prominent role in enabling a Muslim to enter into a closer relationship with God. As previously noted, Sufi practice developed in parallel to canonical Islam. It is a spiritual movement incorporating Sunnis, Shi'as, Ahmadi, and even non-Muslims. Sufism is all-inclusive, trans-sectarian, and transnational. As seekers of truth, Sufis are more open than other Muslims to artistic expression, such as poetry, music, and dance. Music is considered a spiritual discipline in Sufism, and Sufis are considered the musical missionaries of Islam in the Indian subcontinent, playing an essential role in the spread of Islam.

The Sufi practice of *sama'* (literally "hearing" a spiritual musical concert) is a pathway to encounter ecstasy and experience ultimate reality. The term *sama'* means both hearing music and the music that is heard. Sufis center their mystical concerts on an event from Muslim sacred history based on Qur'an Al-Aaraf 7:172, the "primordial covenant" (*mithaq*, referred to in Turkish and Persian texts as the "Day of *Alast*"); during this mythic event from prehistory, all the children of Adam bore witness to Allah's lordship over them.

Sufism's most essential element is the path to the inner soul and pilgrimage to spirituality with sensitivity. Practitioners are more open, compared to the conservative community, to expressions of art that include poetry, music, and dance. In addition, the Sufi devotional genre is woven into emotional feelings and resonates with the shared human experience. Combining all five foundational components of their faith—spirituality, culture, emotions, poetry, and music—Sufis cherish the artistic expressions of the scriptures, particularly the book of Psalms. My personal experience and encounters with Sufi musicians and shrines expand the horizons of psalms for engaging with Muslims in general. The scriptural convergences show striking parallels, in addition to the shared cultural, musical, spiritual, and emotional aspects. These convergences will be discussed in chapter 5.

A *zikr* (*dhikr* in Arabic, meaning "remembrance") is a formulaic phrase that focuses the mind to God and may also bring about an aroused state of consciousness called *hāl* (literally, "condition"). Reciting *ya-Rahman, ya-Rahim* (O All-merciful, O All-compassionate) is a famous *dhikr* from the earliest time. *Du'a* or "supplication" is intimately connected to *dhikr*, such that it is often difficult to make a distinction between the two. Collections of hadiths, both Sunni and Shi'a, devote chapters to the benefits of *du'a* supplication.

Drawing from such practices, prodigious North Indian music and vernacular Sufi poetry create a hybrid-local musical genre: *qawwali*, which conjures the emotion of the divine presence in the human heart. *Qawwali* is one of the popular genres of *zikr* in *sama'* gatherings. Sufis legitimized their *qawwali* singing according to the Qur'an: "So give good tidings to my servants who listen to *al-qaul* [the spoken word] and follow the fairest of it" (Q Al-Zumar 39:17–18). *Qawwali* is the epitome of religious music culture in Pakistan. It is the voice of divine power. At shrines for Chishti and other Sufis in South Asia, devotees make explicit use of symbolism in music. *Qawwali* is considered to be a Sufi devotional genre due to its lyrical poetry. However, it falls into a classical musical category. Nusrat Fateh Ali Khan is a Pakistani *qawwali* singer whose thrilling voice has carried Sufi devotional songs to the world. The primary purpose of such ecstatic singing and dancing is the search for the ultimate, the thirst of the human soul to reach out to its destiny.

Despite the popularity and global acceptance of *qawwali*, Sufis have been criticized and even suffered for their beliefs. Moreover, they are victims of violence from the Salafist/Wahhabist brand of extremist Islam. Whether it is Maulana Rumi of Iran or Bulleh Shah and Shah Latif from Pakistan, the Sufi soul is always longing for the Beloved, the ultimate reality. The artistic expression of music, dance, and instruments is their medium to transport them in the realm of ecstasy to experience their union with the ultimate reality. In the face of the many divisions within the Islamic world, Sufi music is a shared religious spectrum that draws people into relationship across faith boundaries for spiritual nourishment. We will explore this opportunity further in the concluding chapter.

Musical Instruments

With vocal art considered the highest expression of devotion within Islam, the use of instruments in religious music is a contentious subject. Muslim scholars have allowed religious recitation and chanting but barred the use of plucked or stringed instruments as accompaniment. At the same time, percussion from the

Arabic context is permitted. *Daf* (an Arabic drum) is not considered a stringed instrument and is allowed in religious singing and poetry recitation. So the prohibition of *mazamir* (strung) instruments is a cultural restriction. In the Middle Eastern context, stringed instruments are part of the identity of cultural music, so the tension on this topic is high.

Moreover, Islamic ruling is silent about wind instruments. Such instrumental chauvinism raises questions and confusion. If one cultural instrument is allowed, why are others forbidden? Secondly, who prohibited them, and on what authority are they outlawed? Instruments have been marginalized in Islamic practice and considered the devil's invention. Islamic authorities condemning music have linked their attacks against music to its association with entertainment and immorality. Historically, the sharpest attack was against stringed instruments, which symbolized the new art and contributed to pleasure.

Voice remains the chief art and crown of Muslim religious music in Pakistan. All categories of music in the religious realm fall within voice-centric, pitched-sound art. Yet attitudes toward musical instruments continue to evolve. Musically, the whole categories of contemporary noncanonical religious music in Pakistan (as presented above) are based on the Indian raga scale and *taal* rhythms with accompaniment by Indian musical instruments such as the harmonium and barrel drum (*dholak*) or the tabla, especially during *qawwali*. This change is occurring, and even a modern *qawwali* is bringing in new instruments.

***Halal* or *Haram* (Permitted or Prohibited)?**

The canonical and noncanonical music debate is about the permission and prohibition of music in the Muslim context: whether music is *halal* (permitted) or *haram* (prohibited). My research findings confirmed that music has an ambivalent place in Islamic societies. On the broader spectrum of Muslim music culture, at the one end, music is firmly rooted in each sphere of society. On the other end, Islam, in contrast to other faiths such as Hinduism and Christianity, has marginalized and restricted music creativity and practice to the human voice. Religious authorities confront the musical element, and the conservatives look down on musicians. Music has an uncertain status and has become a source of much division in Islam. The creative tension between the practitioners and the pious leads us to the centuries-old controversy among religious academics and artists to find common ground for music in the Muslim context.

The critical and complex issue of the role and status of music in Islam remains controversial. Murtaza Khan Niazi, head of the music academy in Karachi, complains that

> since our early childhood we heard from our imam and muftis that music is *haram* and prohibited and our religion does not permit that. This teaching against music greatly impacted the common Muslim as well as society as a whole. Songs become a symbol of sin in Islamic culture. A common pious Muslim avoided engaging with music, and a few social circles still consider it as a sin.[10]

Niazi's frustration shows the dilemma of the artist community in Pakistan. The rich musical heritage has been moralized; music has become a sign of sin and social stigma. Religious scholars and scribes are afraid of the power of music. Furthermore, "the fear of backlash from both religion and society keeps people away from using music in religion,"[11] Niazi said. Practicing musicians are considered second-class citizens and those who want to practice music are reluctant to engage. Religion and religious leaders can play a pivotal role in either promoting or discouraging music.

Undoubtedly, religious authorities are the main agents curbing classical music in Pakistan and maintaining a general narrative against it.

How does Niazi respond to the question of being a musician? How does he defend his music teaching practice, and how does he counter religious appeals to leave his art? His response is, "our religion is called true faith. Give us a solid reason for the prohibition. Why is it prohibited, and if it is *haram*, then where is the *hurmat* [prohibition] in the Qur'an?"[12]

Musicians and artists are not only defending themselves; they are also well aware of the powerful attraction of music. Niazi argues from the qur'anic perspective and asks for a clear qur'anic injunction. He shared his conversation with a group of Muslim evangelists and argued:

> First of all, if it is prohibited, then where is it? In response to that question, they do not have any substantial documentary evidence and argument, and this matter stays as it is. It seems that they do not have any scriptural evidence, and they do this as their standard practice and disturb musicians from their work.[13]

Due to misunderstanding of the term "music" and selective interpretation of the qur'anic texts, various sects of Muslims historically have adopted a definition constraining the use of music as a means of religious expression. Perhaps they believed that music was so powerfully attached to the emotions and passions, and so overwhelming in its ability to speak and move and enamor people, that it was detrimental to worship of Allah. Another reason behind the antagonism against music developed from the eighth to tenth centuries when the Arab Muslim caliphates were ruling the world and living sinful, materialistic lives with secular entertainments. The religious reformers of that era passed decrees against music and musicians that gradually developed as doctrine and meta-narrative.

The two primary sources to discern the Islamic injunctions on any issue are first the revelation of the Qur'an and then the Hadith/*Sīra*—what the Prophet said and what he practiced. These foremost sources of Islamic Shari'a (law) govern and regulate all aspects of a Muslim's public and private life, including music. The Qur'an, as the revelation of Allah, has the primary and final authority. If the Qur'an is ambiguous, then the second source is the sayings of the Prophet—the collection of Hadith traditions. A third source to discern Islamic injunctions is *fiqh* (Islamic jurisprudence), followed by *ijtihad* (interpretation) and *qiyas* (analogical reasoning). *Fiqh* relates to the teachers of Islamic Shari'a.

The majority of the Sunni Muslim world is divided into four schools of the law, and each has its distinct rulings on specific issues.[14] The scope of my research is restricted to the three main sources of Islamic teaching: the Qur'an, the Hadith, and *fiqh*.

Music and the Qur'an

For the past fourteen centuries, Islam has been divided into two camps on the issue of music. Both camps use qur'anic sources to prove their point. The opponents of music use two qur'anic references to claim that music is prohibited in Islam. The first is Qur'an Luqman 31:6, in which they interpret the word "diverting talk" (Arabic *lahw*) as music: "There are some men who buy diverting talk to lead astray from the way of God." The second passage used to declare that music is *haram* is Qur'an Al-Aaraf 7:32–33. In disputing this interpretation, Mufti Faysal Japanwala, a Muslim scholar, strongly affirms that artistic expression is not prohibited in Islam. "Islam did not prohibit artistic expressions. Allah decreed *haram* only nine things in the Qur'an. Four are related to food, and the five in [Q Al-Aaraf 7:33] are related to our actions towards others. Allah is clear about *haram* things and does not leave that on the scholars or *ijtihad*."[15]

On the issue of *halal* and *haram*, Javed Ahmed Ghamidi[16] and other scholars infer that music is not added in that list (cf. the footnotes of Hadith no. 3). These references clarify that the prohibition of music in Islamic thought has no qur'anic grounds. The Qur'an neither prohibits nor explicitly permits music.

Music in the Hadith Tradition

Because of the ambiguity in qur'anic references, disputants found more substantial support for their positions about music in the authoritative source of the Hadith (also known as the Tradition of the Prophet). The Hadith narrative stands next to the Qur'an as a primary religious resource in Islamic thought. The most definitive collections were compiled by Imam al-Bukhari (d. 870), whose *Sahih Bukhari* is the most famous and frequently quoted by Muslims (*sahih* means genuine). Al-Bukhari, for example, limited the number of traditions he compiled to seven thousand, chosen from among six hundred thousand.

Outside the qur'anic domain, various hadiths and stories were collected about Muhammad's encounter with the common practices of poetry, music, and instrument playing in the Arab peninsula. One of the most famous stories is about the Prophet's welcome to the city of Medina. At the time of the migration, young girls welcomed Rasool Allah (the Messenger of Allah) outside Medina with singing "*Tala' Al Badru 'Alayna*" and playing *daf* (barrel drum). It is considered the most ancient Arab song, and refers to Muhammad as a bright full moon.

Mufti Japanwala narrates another hadith from al-Bukhari about girls playing *daf* and singing a traditional song: "At the occasion of *Eid* [festival], a few girls were singing at Aisha's house, and Rasool was lying on the bed. Abu Bakr stopped them. Nevertheless, Rasool said, let them sing, every nation has a time of *Eid*, and today is their *Eid*."[17] Japanwala also recounted another hadith concerning Muhammad's favorable attitude toward singing: "You came to the house of Aisha and said, Today is a wedding among the Ansar [Medinan natives]. Have you sent a few singing women? She replied, No I did not. Rasool said, It would be good if a few are sent."[18]

Some Hadith references show the acceptance and validity of Arab singing and instrumental music at special occasions such as a wedding, *Eid* (festival), and political or other kinds of communal gatherings, commending the practice of music. These hadiths reflect that Muhammad accepted singing and playing instruments at such occasions. Researchers are finding that the majority of hadiths against music have been fabricated or are otherwise unauthentic.

Fiqh: Teachers of the Law Ruling on Music

In the pursuit of an Islamic ruling on music, we have investigated the two primary sources: the Qur'an and the Hadith. The Qur'an is silent, and the Hadith tradition is fragmented, with most hadiths unauthenticated. Now we come to the third Islamic resource which is *fiqh* (jurisprudence). The *fuqha* (jurist) is always aligning with one of two camps: permissible or prohibited. Muftis Shafi and Usmani of Pakistan say music is prohibited, while Maulana Phoolwari from India favors it. Ghamidi states that music itself is not bad, but if forbidden elements such as adultery are added, then it will be corrupted.[19]

Theologians and jurists have exploited the association of art music with immorality and also linked music to entertainment in attacks against it. Muslim jurists who argue against music are concerned with the moral health of the community. Their arguments do not apply to seekers of Truth. The religious reformer, mystic, and great theologian Abu Hamid al-Ghazali (1058–1111), in his authoritative work *Ihya' Ulum al-Din* (The Revival of the Religious Sciences), attempts to integrate Sufism and orthodoxy. Al-Ghazali concludes that both statutory and analogous evidence indicates the admissibility of music. Al-Ghazali permits music, although under certain circumstances it can be unlawful or undesirable. He also takes each hadith, debates its authenticity, and attempts to conclude that music is not only permitted but *mustehsan* (appreciated and acceptable). In the fourth chapter of his book he provides remarkable pieces of evidence in favor of music.

Al-Ghazali is joined by Mufti Japanwala who asserts: "an external text used in music [can be] lustful or expose one to sexuality; these things can make it wrong."[20] This means that music as a medium is acceptable, but if inappropriate text is added, that will make it forbidden. Due to negative associations of music in the past, early theologians considered music suspect and dangerous to the community of the faithful.

The Status of Music in Islam

Islamic Shari'a allows for four verdicts on the permissibility of human actions such as those corresponding to music:

- *Halal*: legitimate or allowed under religious law.
- *Mubah*: allowed, but looked down on with contempt, as suspect; actions which may be performed, but are not *halal* and therefore are in a lower category.
- *Makruh*: improper, disapproved by religion, but nevertheless not forbidden by Islamic law.
- *Haram*: Forbidden or illicit.

Even so, attempting to apply these verdicts to music does not yield definitive conclusions, because different schools of law interpret the sacred writings in different ways.

Based on this analysis of scholarship as well as those respondents who answered my questions during my research, it is sufficient to say that in general Islam does not prohibit music for religious purposes—it is not *haram*. Theologically, the Qur'an is silent about music, and the interpretation of Hadith and *Sīra* is fragmented. Muslim jurists, muftis, and scholars have their personal preferences about music. In consequence, the community of artists and musicians is suffering due to this confusion.

Ghamidi researched and translated ten Hadiths from Arabic to Urdu from various Hadith collections. His compilation refers to various occasions when Muhammad and his followers encountered musicians, such as weddings, war, traveling, or leisure time at night gathering in the Arabian peninsula. He concludes that music itself is neither *haram* nor abomination, although, due to the power and attraction of music, it could be misused for immorality or adultery.[21]

Because the four leading schools of law in the Islamic world have differences of interpretation, the categorization of various types of music has been the subject of a great legal debate in which there has never been total agreement, except on one point: all lascivious music, which may arouse the lower passions, has been banned by the *ulama* (religious scholars).

Because there is no specific legal sanction against music, and the *ulama* have themselves differed over the centuries as to whether music is *halal* or *haram* according to Shari'a (the Divine Law of Islam), an aura of ambiguity has surrounded the legal status of music since early Islam. This obscurity provides space for music culture to flourish under Islamic law. The arrival of any new form of music from outside the Islamic world has at first caused a great deal of debate. Islam neither prohibited all musical art nor permitted all forms of music; the religious scrutiny is directed toward certain forms of musical practices that are considered to be harmful for aesthetic and moral reasons. This inconsistency and vagueness helped to protect and cultivate music in the Islamic world. There is no central authority or religious hierarchy in Islam. What unites all Muslims is the Qur'an in its Arabic form and the five pillars of the faith.

Both the Hadith and *fiqh* have been used to argue divergent positions about the admissibility of music in Muslim life but no definitive interpretation can be established. While a few Muslim reformers are addressing the issue and clearing the fog around music, these voices are muted and threatened by conservative extremists. This situation gives space for various sects and schools of *fiqh* and Islamic scholars to take their stance on the permission or prohibition of music in the Muslim world.

Moreover, the power of music, as has been noted, can be harnessed for both good and evil. Despite the debate about whether music is *halal* (permissible) or *haram* (prohibited) in Muslim society, Muslim extremists are known to use poetry and music to inspire and motivate young *mujahidin* for jihad.[22] Motivated by this circumstance, Christians desiring to engage their Muslim neighbors in relationships of peace can use musical arts for the opposite purpose.

Listening to music ultimately depends upon human behavior and the state of the heart. The war over music has been fought inside the *dar-ul-Islam* (house of Islam) during the last fourteen centuries, and both fronts are struggling to overcome hurdles. Nevertheless, amid such confusion and chaos, efforts at musical cohesion and collaboration press forward, and practitioners have been using the opportunity to spread the message of interfaith friendship.

Notes

1 Sheema Kermani, personal interview with the author February 19, 2019, in Karachi, Pakistan.

2 Kristina Nelson Davies, "The Qur'an Recited," in *The Middle East*, vol. 6 of *Garland Encyclopedia of World Music,* eds., Virginia Danielson, Scott Marcus, and Dwight Reynolds (New York: Routledge, 2002), 157.

3 Michael Aaron Frishkopf, "Sufism, Ritual, and Modernity in Egypt: Language Performance as an Adaptive Strategy" (PhD diss.,

University of California Los Angeles, 1999), 290. https://sites.ualberta.ca/~michaelf/Frishkopf_dissertation

4 Abdullah Memmon, personal interview with the author March 17, 2019, in Karachi, Pakistan.

5 Memmon, interview.

6 Memmon, interview.

7 Memmon, interview.

8 Mahmood Siddiqui is a chief editor of the magazine *Jamaat-e-Islami* (Muslim Brotherhood), a publication of the largest Muslim political party in Pakistan. This quotation from Siddiqui came during a personal interview with the author February 22, 2019, in Karachi, Pakistan.

9 Mostly, pentatonic ragas such as *shivranjini* (sindhra), *todi*, *marva*, *pooriya dhanasri*, and *ahir bhairav* are used to compose *marsiya*. Presenters of mourning are called *azadar* (mourners of Husain). See https://www.youtube.com/watch?v=2xTlcK9YTx8&t=368s.

10 Murtaza Khan Niazi, personal interview with the author March 19, 2018, in Karachi, Pakistan.

11 Niazi, interview.

12 Niazi, interview.

13 Niazi, interview.

14 The Sunni Muslims give this right of independent reasoning to only four ancient Muslim jurists who lived in the first three centuries of Islam. These four schools of thought are: Hanafi (from Imam Abu Hanifa of Kufa), Maliki (from Imam Malik bin Anas of Medina), Shafi'i (from Imam Muhammad al-Shafi of Medina), and Hanbali (from Imam Ahmad bin Hanbal of Baghdad).

15 Mufti Faysal Japanwala, personal interview with the author February 19, 2019, in Karachi, Pakistan. The list of forbidden things in Qur'an 7:33 includes shameful acts of sin listed in the Qur'an: adultery, stealing, injustice to orphans, liquor, injustice including false testimony, murder, idolatry, stiff-necked disobedience to parents. All these are *haram*, sins forbidden by God. Then there is making any statement about God that is not said or mentioned in the Qur'an. Japanwala noted, "Associating false things to God is also *haram*."

16 Javed Ahmed Ghamidi, personal interview with the author January 8, 2018, in Southern California.

17 Japanwala, interview.

18 Japanwala, interview.

19 Ghamidi, interview.

20 Japanwala, interview.

21 Javed Ahmed Ghamidi, "Ghina and Musiqi," trans. Muhammad Amir (Al-Mawrid: A Foundation for Islamic Research and Education, March 2020), https://www.javedahmedghamidi.org/#!/ishraq/5e537affc824c8e12d5583e6?articleId=5e539c6ec824c8e12d558444&year=2020&decade=2020

22 See, for example, Elisabeth Kendall's essay, "Yemen's Al-Qa'ida and Poetry as a Weapon of Jihad," in *Twenty-First Century Jihad: Law, Society and Military Action*, eds., Elisabeth Kendall and Ewan Stein (London: I. B. Tauris, 2015), 247–69.

5

Convergent Paths
The Psalms and Islam

"*Bismillah al-Rahman al-Rahim*" ("In the name of Allah, the most gracious and merciful")
(Q A-Fatihah 1:1).

From the first chapter of Surah *Al-Fatiha* through the last chapter of Surah *Al-Nas*, all 114 chapters of the Qur'an, with the sole exception of chapter 9, begin with "*Bismillah al-Rahman al-Rahim*"—"In the name of Allah, the most gracious and merciful." This opening invocation is used by every pious Muslim at the initiation of any undertaking. The qur'anic word *bismillah* ("in the name of God") or the full *bismillah al-Rahman al-Rahim* precedes countless daily acts from private to public arenas. Pop musicians even compose songs with this one phrase.

The Qur'an with References to the Bible: A Contemporary Understanding, a collaborative translation with extensive footnotes, cites Zabur/Psalm 103:8 and 145:8 as direct parallels to this opening invocation and its repeated words in verse 3.[1] The same source cites twenty-nine references to passages in the Psalms/Zabur in the footnotes to the second chapter of the Qur'an alone. (See the Appendix for a full chart.)

The Lahore Interfaith Conference of 2019 began with a reading from Psalm 139 and a recitation of the Qur'an from Surah

Al-Rahman ("The Lord of Mercy," Q Al-Rahman 55). The theme of both scripture references was the same: the scriptures converged at the concept of God's creative order and sovereignty over his creation. Other psalm festivals have launched with vocalists singing Psalm/Zabur 40:5–10 or a portion of 69:1–5 in the Raga Bheemplasi, with Muslim and Christian instrumentalists.

These examples hint at the numerous convergences between biblical psalms and the Qur'an, setting the stage for a collaborative Muslim-Christian pilgrimage using the Zabur. This chapter investigates the role and influence of the Psalms in qur'anic understanding and Muslim thought for peacebuilding between Islam and Christianity.

"The Previous Books"

Building bridges of friendship between Christians and Muslims will yield greater fruit when participants understand the Islamic view of what the Qur'an calls "the previous books" or "previous scriptures." As mentioned in chapter 1, the Qur'an teaches its followers to read and respect these books—consisting of the Torah (*Tawrat*), the Psalms (*Zabur*), and the Gospel (*Injil*)—as being sent by God.[2] Muslims believe these three books were revealed by Allah to previous monotheistic religions of Abrahamic faith, and when the Qur'an was revealed it represented the culmination of all prior revelations.

Despite the history of polemical debates and doctrinal differences between Muslims and Christians, the Qur'an, Hadith, and a number of reliable sources from Islamic jurists and scholars have used the Bible to justify Islamic epistemologies, and have even used biblical references in the exegesis of the Qur'an.[3] Some Muslim writers and leaders, including Javed Ahmad Ghamidi, have made it an obligation to read, study, and solidify their understanding of the Bible.[4] Thus, from the Islamic perspective, the Qur'an was sent not to invalidate or abolish the previous or earlier scriptures but to confirm them (see, for instance, Q Yunus 10:37, Q Al-Malaika 35:31–32). The Qur'an strongly affirms that *Allah* is the same God worshiped by faithful Christians, Jews, and Muslims (Q 10:90, 29:46, 73:9).

While the Qur'an mentions the Zabur much less often than the Torah, the importance of the Psalms for the study of the Qur'an has long been recognized in qur'anic scholarship. Angelika Neuwirth's pioneering work is leading the movement to promote the Psalms as pivotal to understanding the compositional nature of some chapters of the Qur'an.[5] She has highlighted abundant parallel structural correspondence and forms of intertextuality between the Psalms and the text of the Qur'an's Meccan surahs.

The participants in my dissertation research showed consensus for a high regard of the Psalms and their primary author, king/prophet David. Both Sufis and other scholar participants perceive the Psalms in the same monotheistic chain of divine revelation as the Qur'an, despite Christians denying the claim. The Hadith tradition continues the logic, viewing King David as a prophet, and treats the Zabur (Psalms) in the piety model of Islamic thought.

Almost every participant agreed that the Psalms can promote peace and interfaith friendship between Muslims and Christians without any theological or doctrinal adjustments. They believe music and psalms together create bonds deeper than mere friendship, strengthening collaborative efforts that bring together the faith traditions. Follow-up questions were designed to gauge the singers' and scholars' views about the status of psalms and how respondents trust psalms to provide guidance, their response when they hear them, and how close they feel to their religion as a result. Singers and scholars mostly agree that the Psalms are friendly toward the felt needs of the ordinary person.

My research revealed convergences between the Qur'an and the Psalms that I have grouped into five categories I call the five

"Rs"—Revelation, Recitation, Ritual, Reconciliation, Relational—plus an "S" for Spiritual convergences. We will look at each of these in turn.

Revelation Convergences

The first striking convergence point between the Psalms and the Qur'an is that both are considered as revelation from the same divine source. As mentioned above, the Qur'an does not make any distinction about the origin of previous revelations, identifying them all as divinely sent.

To believe in Allah's revealed books, which include the Psalms of David, is one of the foundational elements of the Islamic faith system (*arkan-e-Iman*). The Qur'an cites three sections of the Bible: the Pentateuch, or Books of Moses (*Tawrat*); the Psalms of David (*Zabur*); and the Gospels of Jesus (*Injil*). Qur'an Hud 11:17 declares that the Book of Moses is an *Imam-e-Rehman* (leader of mercy), and the Tawrat, Zabur, and Injil are mentioned several times as the *kalam-e-Allah* (the word of God) that contains "light" (*noor*) and "instructions" (*hidayat*). Qur'an Mariam 19:33 mentions Jesus's birth, death, and resurrection. Notable qur'anic references to the Bible include:

> O you who have believed, believe in Allah and His Messenger and the Book that He sent down upon His Messenger and the Scripture which He sent down before. And whoever disbelieves in Allah, His angels, His books, His messengers, and the Last Day has certainly gone far astray. (Q Al-Nisa 4:136)

> So if you are in doubt, [O Muhammad], about that which We have revealed to you, then ask those who have been reading the Scripture before you. The truth has certainly

come to you from your Lord, so never be among the doubters. (Q Yunus 10:94)

During an interview I conducted with Rehan Yousufi, an Islamic researcher and scholar, he asserted:

> Islam sees these sacred scriptures as springing out of the same source. Allah is clear that it is a part of our faith to believe in these books; they contain blessing, light, and guidance. These books descended on prophets, and as we believe in the prophet Muhammad and the Qur'an, we also believe in these previous scriptures. We will not consider being a Muslim by definition if we do not have faith in these previous scriptures. Qur'an sees these scriptures from this point of view. Whether it is *Tawrat*, *Zabur*, or *Injil*, believing in these scriptures is a part of our salvation. So, Qur'an gives this status to these books.[6]

Yousufi went on to say "the invitation of the Qur'an is that this book [Zabur] is a part of the continuous tradition." Other interviewees during my dissertation research repeatedly said that if Muslims believe in the Qur'an, then they should believe in the "previous scriptures" as well, linking them to the same divine source.

Moreover, one of my research interviewees, Farman Ali, a Muslim scholar in Lahore, told me that in the Hadith collection of *Sahih Bukhari*, the word *Zabur* is used as an alternative term synonymous with the Qur'an. Bukhari was referring to the Psalms when he used the word *Qur'an*; our translators put the word *Zabur* in square brackets.[7]

Scholars have explored various qur'anic references pointing to the Psalms. They observe a parallel correlation and similar literary features between the individual chapters of the Qur'an and the Psalms of the same title number. For the present study, I share the following three qur'anic references as they have been discussed in the broader scholarly arena:

> Indeed, We have revealed to you, [O Muhammad], We revealed to Noah and the prophets after him. And We revealed to Abraham, Ishmael, Isaac, Jacob, the Descendants, Jesus, Job, Jonah, Aaron, and Solomon, and to David We gave the Book [Zabur]. (Q Al-Nisa 4:163)

> And your Lord is most knowing of whoever is in the heavens and the earth. And We have made some of the prophets exceed others [in various ways], and to David We gave the Book [Zabur]. (Q Al-Isra 17:55)

> And We have already written in the Book [Zabur] after the [previous] mention that the land [of Paradise] is inherited by My righteous servants. (Q Al-Anbiya 21:105)

Concerning this last reference, another translation of Qur'an Al-Anbiya 21:105 says, "We have already written in the Psalms, the book of remembrance, that 'My righteous servants will inherit the earth.'" Some Muslim scholars think this verse refers to Exodus 32:13, "it [the land] will be their inheritance forever." Others agree that Qur'an 21:105 is a validation of Psalm 37, and consider the qur'anic reference a direct quotation from verses 11 and 29: "The meek will inherit the land and enjoy peace and prosperity" and "The righteous will inherit the land and dwell in it forever."

While these references to the Psalms in the Qur'an pertain to the Psalms of David and have attracted various scholars in Islamic history, they are still unknown to most of the Muslim society in Pakistan. Here is another opportunity for bridge building waiting to be explored.

Recitation Convergences

The Qur'an is essentially an oral document. It was first a recitation and only later a written book. The mode of recitation was revealed to the Messenger himself in the Qur'an (Q Al-Qiyamah 75:16–19). Religious scholars relate vocal art to scriptural recitation. Unaccompanied vocal art in recitation of sacred scripture is considered a blessing and respected in the music culture.

The Qur'an's vocal presence in the Muslim community is keenly felt, more pervasive than even ritual, devotional life, or public life. Recitation of qur'anic verses takes place during all ritual expressions including *salat* (daily prayers) and the *hajj* (pilgrimage to Mecca) as well as at every formal occasion, such as the signing of a wedding contract, the closing of an agreement, prayer (*du'a*) at a tomb, and many more everyday occasions in society. From birth to death, virtually every action a Muslim takes is potentially accompanied by the spoken words of the Qur'an.

During the past fourteen centuries, the Qur'an has been learned, read, and passed on by vocal repetition and memorization. The word for "book" in Islam, *kitab*, is ultimately not a written manuscript but a holy "reciting" or "recitation," which is precisely what the Arabic word *qur'an* means. "Qur'an" is a verbal noun from the root meaning "to recite, read aloud." Even after its codification as a single, composite book of revelations, it is as a recited text that the Qur'an has played its central role in Muslim piety and practice.

Regardless of their native vernacular, Muslims recite and memorize the Qur'an in Arabic and *tilawat* (sacred recitation) of the Qur'an is done without any instrumental accompaniment. A Hadith of the Prophet declares, "God has said, 'Whoever is so absorbed in reciting the Qur'an that he is distracted from praying to Me and asking [things] of Me, him I shall give the best reward [that is granted to] those who are grateful.'"

The style of Arabic in which the Qur'an was written is rhymed prose. The very name "al-Qur'an" (the Recitation) underscores how the qur'anic revelations were initially wholly oral texts intended to be rehearsed and recited, first by Muhammad, then by the faithful. It was not sent as "writing on parchments," as Qur'an Al-Anam 6:7 states. Recitation or cantillation of the Qur'an is the most popular activity in Muslim piety, being carried out even in competitions. *Hafiz-Qur'an* (those who recite by memory, having memorized the entire book) and *qari* (reciters and chanters) are held in high esteem in the Muslim world. According to Muslims, Arabic is the sacred language of God as well as Islam.

In general, the psalms compiled in the scriptures were composed not only as poetry but as lyrics to songs, and so were meant to be vocalized and heard aloud. Like the Qur'an, then, they were intended as divine revelation for education and guidance, delivered in oral form. The Apostle Paul affirms the didactic and divine purposes of the Psalms in his letters to the Ephesians ("speaking to one another with psalms, hymns, and songs from the Spirit," 5:19) and Colossians ("Let the message of Christ dwell among you richly as you teach and admonish one another with all wisdom through psalms, hymns, and songs from the Spirit," 3:17). Thus Christians sing psalms and play musical instruments in their worship.

The Psalms and the Qur'an also converge with each other as poetic text. While many Muslims would deny that the Qur'an is poetry, they acknowledge it contains a poetic structure. Both the Psalms and the Qur'an are recited as a ritual performance in private and public piety, and both books are compiled in nonchronological order.

From a literary and sonic framework, the Psalms and the Qur'an stand closely on similar ground. In an oral culture, song stories are a powerful tool to keep traditions alive. Consequently, an Islamic musical form such as *qasida*, *hamd* (hymn), or *qawwali* composed using scripture from the Zabur would serve as a bridge to connect Islam and Christianity for peacebuilding and social harmony. With the Qur'an and the Zabur converging as revelation, their tandem recitation can enhance prophetic peacemaking among Muslims and Christians in Pakistan and beyond.

Ritual Convergences

I am defining ritual here as the action that emerges from valuing revelation and recitation. Islamic worship and piety is based on the five "pillars of the religion" (*arkan al-din*) obligatory for every faithful Muslim. These five rituals are *shahadah* (witnessing to the oneness of God and the prophet Muhammad), *salat* (five canonical daily prayers), *zakah* (almsgiving), *sawm* (fasting during the month of Ramadan), and *hajj* (performance of the annual pilgrimage to Mecca). For our purposes, only two of these five rituals—*salat* prayers and the *hajj* pilgrimage—will be discussed in terms of convergences between the Psalms and Islam, along with one more ritual practice. The communal ceremonial life of a devout Muslim consists of daily religious rituals incorporating, for instance, repentance, lament, and burial practices, although the Sufi path gives less consideration to the external ritual and emphasizes inner spirituality.

Salat: Canonical Prayer

Qur'anic passages are central to Muslims' five times of *namaz* (prayer) each day. A few striking parallels can be observed between the practice of these ritual prayers and practices mentioned in the Psalms.

Ablution: Before offering prayers, Muslims perform a ritual cleansing of the physical body, involving washing the hands, rinsing the mouth and nostrils, then washing the face, forearms, head, ears, and feet. This ablution compares to the ancient monastic practice from the sixth century CE of praying the Seven Penitential Psalms (Pss 6, 32, 38, 51, 102, 130, 143) to aid spiritual cleansing of the human soul. This practice was often combined with sacred physical motions and a ritual bath using holy water to purify the soul. Psalm 51:7–10 in particular runs parallel for spiritual purity and cleanliness: "Purge me with hyssop, and I shall be clean; wash me, and I shall be whiter than snow" (v. 7).

Time: *Salat* prayers are to be performed just before dawn, at noon, in midafternoon, just after sunset, and in the evening. Likewise, Psalm 51:17 says, "Evening and morning, and at noon, will I pray and cry aloud: and he shall hear my voice." In addition, Friday is considered a sabbath in Islam, and it is a sign of public piety and obligatory for a male Muslim to join in congregational prayer in the mosque at noontime on Fridays. This practice probably finds a parallel in what have been called the Sabbath Psalms (Pss 29, 92, 93, 95–99) due to their use in the synagogue.

Direction: Muslim prayers must be made in the direction of Mecca and carried out in a state of ritual purity. In the same way, Psalm 138:2 declares, "I will worship toward thy holy temple."

Postures: Islamic practice echoes several postures mentioned in the Psalms. These include: raising the hands to the ears ("the lifting up of my hands as the evening offering" Ps 141:2); bowing ("I will bow in reverence for You"—Ps 5:7); lifting eyes to heaven ("I lift my eyes to the hills. From where does my help come? My help comes from the Lord, who made heaven and earth" Ps121:1–2); and sitting in silence ("Be still, and know that I am God" Ps 46:10).

Hajj: Pilgrimage

The fifth of the fundamental Muslim ritual practices, or "pillars" of Islam, is the *hajj*, an annual pilgrimage to Mecca every adult Muslim is expected to perform at least once in a lifetime. According to the pilgrimage ritual, the *hajj* has two phases: First, after entering Mecca, a devotee walks seven times around the Ka'aba, kisses or touches the Black Stone, prays twice, and runs seven times between two small hills. In the second phase of the ritual, animals are sacrificed in commemoration of the Abrahamic sacrifice of his son.

Regarding a parallel with the Psalms, the Hebrew tradition has arranged a set of fifteen psalms called the Psalms (or Songs) of Ascent. These psalms (Pss 120–34) were intended to be sung by pilgrims on their way to Mount Zion, ascending to the entrance of the city gates of Jerusalem and then to the steps of the Temple.

There is another controversial yet common parallel reference concerning pilgrimage. Psalm 84:6 says, "As they pass through the Valley of Bakka, they make it a place of springs." Qur'an Aali Imran 3:96 reads, "Lo! the first Sanctuary appointed for mankind was that at Becca, a blessed place, a guidance to the peoples." Muslim tradition may refer the word Bakka to the city Mecca, and asserts that this passage from Psalms is a description of pilgrims going to Mecca for the *hajj*. They identify the well or springs of this verse with the well Zam-zam, which has ritual significance during the *hajj*. While the claim of identifying Bakka ("valley of weeping") with the city of Mecca is debatable,[8] the convergence point of Psalm 84:6 to both traditions is the reference to a pilgrimage to the house of God and His providence amid harsh travel terrain.

Lament, Repentance, and Loss

Lament in both Christian and Muslim traditions can be considered a ritual practice and a parallel point of comparison between the Psalms and the Qur'an. The practice of lament in terms of sin, repentance, and seeking forgiveness has not been emphasized in many Christian communities, although mourning and lamenting is both biblical and human. Many Muslims, on the other hand, feel a close connection to the prophet David and his penitential character when he expresses lament in Psalm 51. Thus the lament psalms can serve as a way for Christians in Pakistan and other Muslim nations to reconnect with their majority neighbors. For instance, Psalm 74 is a lament by Asaph, the Levitical singer and worship leader. He leads in the transition from *dukh/dard* (grief/pain/anguish) to *sukh/iman* (belief/faith) and takes the devotee to the point of *du'a/dava* (plea/remedy) in the midst of chaos and confusion.

Another qur'anic reference, Qur'an Hud 11:52, says "ask forgiveness of your Lord and then repent to Him. He will send [rain from] the sky upon you in showers and increase you in strength [added] to your strength." This verse calls to mind the prayer of Solomon at the dedication of the first temple in 2 Chronicles 7:14: "If my people, which are called by my name, shall humble themselves, and pray, and seek my face, and turn from their wicked ways; then will I hear from heaven, and will forgive their sin, and will heal their land" (KJV). It also echoes Psalm 84:7: "They go from strength to strength, till each appears before God in Zion."

Lament is appropriate with any kind of loss. In connecting the psalms of lament to the Muslim context, there is a clear link to Shi'a Muslim mourning practices when they pay homage to their saint by crying out "Ali, Ali," singing *manqabat*, or when they perform *ta'zia*, mourning in commemoration of the massacre at Karbala. Mourning and lament bring people together whenever human beings feel compassion for those who are suffering.

Death and the loss of loved ones are sorrows common to every human experience. The second chapter of the Qur'an refers to a recitation at funerals or upon hearing about the death of a loved one. A Muslim is commanded to recite *Al-Istirja*—"Indeed we belong to Allah, and indeed to Him we will return" (Q Al Buqarah 2:156)—as an expression of trust and faith in God at the news of a death and an expression of deep sorrow at the loss of a loved one. Surah 36, *Ya Sin*, is often recited at burials, or on the approach of death. The dying person is instructed to say the *shahadah-la ilaha illallah* ("There is no god but Allah").

In Luke 23:46, Jesus during his crucifixion recites from Psalm 31:5: "Into your hands I commit my spirit; deliver me, Lord, my faithful God" (NIV). The same concept is found in Psalm 4:8: "In peace I will lie down and sleep, for you alone, Lord, make me dwell in safety" (NIV). Another reference says, "because you will not abandon me to the realm of the dead, nor will you let your faithful one see decay" (Psalm 16:10, NIV), an assurance of protection and comfort at the time of death. "Faithful one" is an active term whereby the subject decides to entrust or give over his soul into the hands of the heavenly creator.

Mahboob M. Noble, a Presbyterian minister from the Church of Scotland, sees an emotional expression of lament in Pakistan's society. He observes that social crisis, human misery, and pain can forge a strong bond between humans who have shared the same chaos in their lives. He points to the psalms of lament and their relationship to Pakistani society:

> In the Pakistani context, judicial, political, and social injustice is rampaging, and lament psalms are essential to address such a situation. Secondly, lament psalms invite us to show empathy to other suffering persons. They invite us to feel their pain and vice versa. In this regard, they make us sensitive to each other. Our sensitivity to others helps us to promote peace and harmony.[9]

These Psalms of David are personal prayers that resonate with Muslim practice as an assurance and hope for a protection hereafter. Reciting these psalms as a prayer is a sign of depositing trust for protection at the time of departure from the body. No doubt, the same is true in Christian teachings as well. Human emotions cannot be controlled at such a moment.

Reconciliation Convergences

The qur'anic virtue of reconciliation is both vertical and horizontal: reconciliation takes place between humans and God, as well as between individuals and other people. In Islamic thought, all merit boils down to these two merits. Qur'an Al Nisa 4:114 asserts, "No good is there in much of their private conversation, except for those who enjoin charity or that which is right or conciliation between people. And whoever does that, seeking means to the approval of Allah—then We are going to give him a great reward."

Qur'an Al-Anfal 8:1 states, "So fear Allah and amend that which is between you, and obey Allah and His Messenger, if you should be believers." The settlement of disagreement is a high virtue in Islam: "there is no sin upon them if they make terms of the settlement between them—and settlement is best" (Q Al Nisa 4:128). Another reference evokes justice: "Then make settlement between them in justice and act justly. Indeed, Allah loves those who act justly" (Q Al-Hujurat 49:9). Based on this verse, the Qur'an invites the peacemakers to step in and mediate between the two parties to endeavor to forge reconciliation and bring peace. Thus, the reason for the qur'anic insistence on reconciliation is coupled with equity in the verse under consideration. According to Hadith tradition, the best horizontal action toward human beings is *sadaqa* (charity), and the second virtue is settling disputes between people.

The reconciliation concept underlines the internal struggle of the House of Islam: militancy vs. modernity, radical vs. relational approaches, confrontation vs. reconciliation. In the face of radical and militant Islam, reconciliation brings a liberal, tolerant, and moderate faith. The qur'anic perspective on reconciliation unmasks the extremists' deliberate misinterpretation of the Qur'an. Reconciliation is the only solution to bridge the widening chasm between the West and the Muslim world.

Pakistan's first female prime minister, Benazir Bhutto, wrote a book published after her assassination entitled *Reconciliation*, which lays out her vision of Islam as "an open, pluralistic and tolerant religion."[10] She offers a moderate and tolerant face of Islam to curb the tide of Islamic terrorism in Pakistan and across the globe. She calls for revival of the values of tolerance and justice that she sees lying at the heart of her religion. She refers to a passage from Qur'an Al-Kafirun 109:6—"You shall have your religion, and I shall have my religion"—in support of her argument that Islam preaches tolerance and pluralism. Bhutto's vision of reconciliation expands and covers both the political and the religious spectrums between the Muslim world and the West.

My research participants make clear that reconciliation as a relational process points to both vertical (Holy One) and horizontal (human) relationships. The Psalms propose reconciliation in Psalms 66, 67, and 68, among other passages. Psalm 103:10–12 highlights vertical reconciliation as it reminds us that our sins are removed as far as the east is from the west. Psalm 103:10 says, "He has not dealt with us after our sins nor rewarded us according to our iniquities." Moreover, horizontal reconciliation is unattainable if vertical reconciliation is not attempted. Reconciliation builds relationships, another category of convergence discussed in the following section.

Relational Convergences

Many passages in the Psalms as well as in the Qur'an and Hadith talk about the dynamics of relationships, including relations between and among humans as well as relations between humankind and God, both individually and corporately. The descriptions in the Zabur of the faith and thirst of the lover of God touch Muslim hearts. Rehan Yousufi, an Islamic researcher and scholar I interviewed, noted how "personal relationship is highlighted in the Zabur," and told me:

> Whenever I am in crisis, I read Zabur. In crisis and critical situations, God himself comes down on earth in his

> distress. This personal relation in the Zabur is phenomenal. If any assurance on a deep and personal level full of hope, love, and assurance is available in the world, that is only in the book of Psalms.[11]

In addition, several human-felt needs are expressed and acknowledged in both the Psalms and the Qur'an. Among them are prayer, praise, protection, and patience.

Prayer (*du'a*) is a powerful expression of faith in the Muslim context. The most prominent source from early Islam, *The Psalms of Islam: Al-Sahifat Al-Sajjadiyya*, is the oldest prayer manual and one of the most seminal works of Islamic spirituality. Various honorifics in *fiqh Jafferia* (from the Shi'a tradition) also call it "Sister of the Qur'an," "Gospel of the Folk of the House," and "Psalms of the Household of Muhammad." These prayers are composed by Zayn al-Abidin (d. 95 AH/713 CE), "the fourth of the Shi'ite Imams, after his father Husayn, his uncle Hasan, and his grandfather Ali, the Prophet's son-in-law. Shi'ite tradition considers the *Sahifa* a book worthy of the utmost veneration, ranking it behind only the Qur'an and Ali's *Nahj al-balagha*."[12]

Praise (*tasbih*) is a sign of public piety in the Pakistani context. Short qur'anic phrases are used in adoration, glorification, and celebration of Allah. For instance:

> *subhan-Allah*: (glory to Allah) (from Q Al-Isra 17:43)
> *insha-Allah*: (if Allah wills, God willing)
> *mā shā'-llāh*: (whatever Allah wills) (from Q Al Kahf 18: 39)
> *al-hamdu lillah*: (praise be to Allah) (from Q Al-Fatihah 1:2)
> *Allahu akbar*: (Allah is greater)

These phrases punctuate Muslim speech, even outside of the Arabic-speaking world, as do qur'anic expressions invoking God's mercy (*rahmah*) or seeking forgiveness (*istighfar*). Another surah,

"Unity" or "Purity" (Q Al-Ikhlas 112), serves as the basis for many litanies of praise.

Protection is another felt need linking the Psalms and the Qur'an. During the Covid-19 pandemic, every faith tradition, including those in Pakistan's religious realm, responded to the fear of the virus's risk to global health. Psalm 91 and its prayer of protection went viral on social media. Moreover, in the Pakistani context, five other Psalms (29, 45, 64, 65, and 78) may resonate to protect oneself or one's home from evil, or for a number of other mundane needs. Praying the Psalms provides a sense of protection and security to the weary soul. People need assurance of protection from the evil eye and bad omens; in addition, having good fortune, finding a suitable life partner, and bearing a child are everyday felt needs in Pakistani society. Two surahs that "deliver from evil" (Q Al-Falaq 113 and Q Al-Nas 114, known collectively as *al-Mu'awwidhatan*) are used extensively as talismanic recitations. Others are often recited before going to bed or sleep, particularly the powerful and moving strains. The most popular are the "Throne Verse" of Q Al-Baqarah 2:255 and the surah of the "Light" (Q Al-Noor 24).

Additionally, Hadith tradition requires for *du'a* the *salat al-Musafir*, which is a prayer for travel mercies. The travel prayer invites God to keep the supplicants safe as soon as they start their travels and also when arriving back home safely. The prayer and invocation of travel and protection resonate with the theme in Psalm 121:7–8 ("The Lord will keep you from all harm—he will watch over your life; the Lord will watch over your coming and going both now and forevermore.") Furthermore, at the communal level, various short qur'anic phrases are part of regular life. Whether it is a wedding, house construction, birth, social or sacred festivals, purchasing a new home or vehicle, job, or any activity related to a person, family, or community, sacred prayers are recited.

Patience is another virtue upheld in the Qur'an: "Verily I will test you with fear and hunger, and loss of wealth, life, and the fruit (of your labor), so give glad tidings to the patient ones" (Q Al-Baqarah 2:155). Psalm 40:1 also reminds us to be patient, and resonates with the same assurance to those who wait patiently for the Lord.

Personal relationship with God is possible through the scriptures that include the Psalms/Zabur and the Qur'an. In particular, Sufis develop an intimate relationship with God through spiritual practices, and we turn now to look at more parallels between the Psalms and Sufi Islam.

Spiritual Convergences: Psalms and the Sufi Path

Sufism, as an interior journey, has long emphasized personal spirituality and devotion. Exploring the Sufi path, I had the privilege to interview three Sufi scholars who study the Shah Abdul Latif Bhittai (1689–1752 CE), an eminent Sufi laureate from Sindh in what is now Pakistan. These representatives of Sindhi Sufi spirituality and scholarship gave valuable help in understanding the teachings of Sufism.

Sufism has spread a message of love, peace, and harmony in the province of Sindh. Sher Mehrani, a professor of Sufism at Karachi University, shared the history of Sufism in Sindh and has made a distinguished contribution to the study of Shah Latif in this region. The spiritual convergences of the Psalms and Sufis reveal conscious cognitive creativity, and emotional and devotional connectivity. These convergences focus on inner purity as well as pathways through music and scriptural encounters for interfaith friendship.

The prophet Muhammad's mystical experience forms the foundation of mysticism or Sufism in Islam. Furthermore, Ali,

Muhammad's cousin and son-in-law, is considered as being an *Imam-e-Sufiya*, a leader of Sufis. Professor Mehrani describes the Sufi goal of *tasavvuf*, the pathway to encounter ecstasy and experience ultimate reality:

> Self-awareness is a way to *tasavvuf*. When walking to that path, then the negativity of extremisms and suicidal thoughts are erased from the human mind. The state of self-awareness comes when a person detaches himself from his body.[13]

Mehrani quotes another couplet: "Why are you going far in search of God? Why are you not finding [him] inside you?" (my translation). He continues, "If you look at your inside, God resides inside you. When he is residing inside you, there is no need to search outside. It is the destiny of Sufism."

Psalm 139 and Sufi Poetry

Psalm 139 shows particular convergence points with Islam. While listening to the Urdu words *aasman* (heavens) and *pataal* (underground/depth) in this psalm, Professor Mehrani made a few connections of similarities between Shah Latif's poetry and Psalm 139. For instance, he describes the "depths" in Latif's poetry: "The lotus is in the depth, but the *bhanwra* (bumble-bee) is from the sky," and explains, "Who arranged their meetings? One is rooted in depths, and others flying in the sky. Who joined them together? It is spirituality and love that binds them together" (my translation).[14]

Mehrani's understanding from Shah Latif's poetry of the inner search and God's presence at every place resonates with Psalm 139:7–12. The psalmist shares the same concept of God's omnipresence in the cosmic order: "Where can I go from your Spirit? Where can I flee from your presence? If I go up to the heavens, you are there; if I make my bed in the depths, you are there" (vv. 7–8). Thus the two traditions merge into one expression of praise that raises the spirits of Muslim and Christian alike.

Music, Dance, and Harmony

Music and dance play important roles in Sufi spirituality. Mehrani believes that in Turkish Sufism, Maulana Rumi and his *Raqs-e-Bismil* whirling dervish dance are reflected in Shah Latif's poetry. The Bible also portrays David as a singer, prophet, and dancer (1 Chr 23:5, Amos 6:5, 2 Sam 6:14). There are many references in the Psalms to singing songs (22:22; 47:6; 96; 100; 104:33, for example), and dancing (30:11–12; 149:3–4; 150:4). For musical instruments, the book of Psalms categorizes these in three types: stringed (33:2; 43:4; 57:8; 71:22; 81:2; 92:3; 98:5, for example), wind (47:5; 81:3; 98:6; 150:3) and percussion (68:25; 81:2; 149:3; 150:4). All are in evidence at the interfaith music festivals I have helped arrange in Pakistan. Muslim and Christian musicians, singers, and scholars alike express Sufi ideals which, in turn, reflect Christian belief and practice.

Sufi thought also recognizes and honors the universality of friendship and harmony. Sher Mehrani quoted part of a poem from Shah Latif, which starts with references to India, Afghanistan, and China; at the end Latif prays, "O my Lord, keep these countries flourishing, [that] Not only Sindh, but the whole world may live in peace" (my translation).

In a similar vein, Psalm 60:6–8 talks about the rule of God over neighbor territories, while Psalm 87:4–7 converges with the same idea of universal connection:

> Glorious things are said of you, city of God:
> "I will record Rahab and Babylon among those who acknowledge me—
> Philistia too, and Tyre, along with Cush—and will say, 'This one was born in Zion.'"

> Indeed, of Zion it will be said, "This one and that one were born in her, and the Most High himself will establish her."
> The Lord will write in the register of the peoples: "This one was born in Zion."
> As they make music they will sing, "All my fountains are in you."

Amidst my conversations with Sufi scholars, I read Psalm 42 from the Urdu Bible. After listening to verse 1 ("As the deer pants for streams of water, so my soul pants for you, my God"), Mehrani quoted Latif's couplet that mentions the search of a male deer using the metaphor of deer musk:

> "As a deer runs into the desert for the aroma of *musk*'" [deer musk, or *kasturi* in India]: The deer is unaware that the smell is coming from his own body. The deer runs to find that musk outside, while the aroma which the deer is searching for is already inside him.[15]

A musk deer running in search of his aroma paints a vivid image of the inner path of a human soul thirsting in search for God. The female deer of Psalm 42:1 thirsts for the water, and in the Pakistani context the male deer searches for the musk aroma, a parallel metaphor connecting the Psalms and Sufi ideas. The concepts of spiritual thirst, quest/pilgrimage, and the deer image are convergence points. Mehrani shared about enculturation within Sufism:

> Mostly Sufis came from outside; for instance, Latif came from Harrat, Afghanistan, and adapted the culture, and the culture adopted him. Later he became an icon of love and peace. Zia Abrro shared that there is no restriction

> of religion at the Shah Latif shrine. The most prominent religion is humanity, and if we know humanity, then we are Sufi. *Tasavvuf* is not a religion but a school of thought in every religion.[16]

Strongly emphasizing convergences between the Abrahamic faiths, Mehrani said, "Hazrat Dawood (AS) [David] who received the book of Zabur is ours as well. Hazrat Muhammad is yours and Hazrat Essa [Jesus] is ours as well. We all meet each other at one point. Denominational institutions have created the divisions. The exercise of power and authority is drifting us away from the message of love and unity." Explicitly pointing to the musical and poetical convergences in the cultural context, Mehrani continued, "This school of thought consists of love, harmony, spirituality, and all these elements mixed in [music and poetry]. . . . Christian mysticism is a whole universe of love, respect, and harmony. God's Spirit is moving in every human being."[17]

Challenges and Opportunities

Clearly, the Qur'an can be considered a gateway to the Psalms. Both of the Islamic primary sources, the Qur'an and Hadith, endorse the Psalms/Zabur as divine revelation and consider this book in the same revelatory chain. The Christian concept, of course, sees the book of Psalms as divine scripture but differs entirely from the Muslim view of continuing and culminating revelation in the Qur'an.

Herein lies a significant challenge for using the Psalms/Zabur in interfaith bridge-building efforts. Most Muslims neither read nor recite Psalms as a separate book, but instead believe the "previous books" later emerged in the Qur'an; thus, they do not need to read any other divine book, even though the Qur'an affirms them. Rehan Yousufi, one of the Islamic scholars I interviewed, confessed, "The problem in the Muslim tradition is that they do not read or respect [even] the Qur'an. How can they read previous books?"

Despite such pessimism, however, my research respondents agreed that reciting the Psalms in line with qur'anic tradition has the ability to contribute to meaningful interaction between Muslim and Christian communities, bringing them into a single space for mutual worship and adoration of *Allah* who has revealed himself. Especially when combined with contextual musical forms, such recitation of revealed scripture can promote reconciliation and relational convergence.

Rehan Yousufi, one of the scholars I interviewed, stated that "Psalms have a distinct structure of prayer and praise, and the Qur'an has a psalm style as well. The fundamental surah of the Qur'an [Surah Al-Fatiha, the first] has copied the psalms pattern. Surah Fatiha is a psalms style."[18] With this in mind, let us look closely at this first chapter of the Qur'an, which serves as its preface. It resonates in every prayer of Muslims, as it is an integral part of each of the five daily ritual prayers.

Bismillah ar-Rahman ar-Raheem
Al hamdu lillaahi rabbil 'alameen
Ar-Rahman ar-Raheem
Maaliki yaumid Deen
Iyyaaka na'abudu wa iyyaaka nasta'een
Ihdinas siraatal mustaqeem
Siraatal ladheena an 'amta' alaihim, Ghairil maghduubi' alaihim waladaaleen
Aameen

In the name of God, the infinitely Compassionate and Merciful.
Praise be to God, Lord of all the worlds.

The Compassionate, the Merciful.
Ruler on the Day of Reckoning.
You alone do we worship, and You alone do we ask for help.
Guide us on the straight path,
The path of those who have received your grace; not the way of those who have brought down wrath, nor of those who wander astray.
Amen.

"O Allah, guide us on the straight path" is thus a key petition of Muslims everywhere. As Christians, we can heartily pray this prayer along with them.

Notes

1 Safi Kaskas and David Hungerford, *The Qur'an with References to the Bible: A Contemporary Understanding* (Fairfax, VA: Bridges of Reconciliation, 2016), 1.

2 Qur'anic passages identifying the previous scriptures as given by God (and in some instances explicitly urging belief in them) include Q Al-Baqarah 2:53, 87; Q Aali Imran 3:3–4, 47–48; Q Al-Nisa 4:47, 136, 163; Q Al-Maidah 5:46–48, 66; Q Al-Annam 6:154–6; Q Yunus 10:37, 94; Q Al-Isra 17:55; Q Al-Anbiya 21:105; Q Al Muminun 23:49; Q Al-Fruqan 25:35; Q Al Malaika 35:31–32; Q Al-Suffat 37:114–18; Q Al Mumin 40:53; Q Al Ahqaf 46:12; Q Al-Hadid 57:27; Q Al Ala 87:18–19.

3 See, for example: Walid A. Saleh, "A Fifteenth-Century Muslim Hebraist: Al-Biqāʿī and His Defense of Using the Bible to Interpret the Qurʾān." *Speculum* 83 (2008), 629–54.

4 Javed Ahmed Ghamidi, personal interview with the author January 8, 2018, in Southern California.

5 See, for example: "The 'Late Antique Qur'an': Jewish-Christian Liturgy, Hellenic Rhetoric, and Arabic Language." (Public lecture by Angelika Neuwirth, June 3, 2009. Institute for Advanced Study). https://www.youtube.com/watch?v=qHCeYSvazY4. See also, Angelika Neuwirth,

"Qur'anic Readings of the Psalms," in *The Qur'ān in Context: Historical and Literary Investigation into the Qur'ānic Milieu*, eds., Angelika Neuwirth, Nicolai Sinai, and Michael Marx (Leiden, Netherlands: Brill Publishers, 2010), 733–78.

6 Rehan Yousufi, personal interview with the author February 20, 2019, in Karachi, Pakistan.

7 Farman Ali, personal interview with the author February 16, 2019, in Lahore, Pakistan. The Hadith reference from *Sahih Bukhari* about the synonymy of "Psalm" and the Qur'an is #3417. Thank you very much, Farman, and clapping. See https://www.youtube.com/watch?v=Ughxhv_EQ58 for an Urdu narration of Hadith 3417.

8 See my 2020 video posting on my Eric Sarwar YouTube channel: "Valley of Baca: An Exploration of the Psalm (84:5–6) and its relation to the House of God." https://www.youtube.com/watch?v=3ntFI-k9q1g&t=14s

9 Mahboob M. Noble, personal interview with the author February 16, 2019, in Lahore, Pakistan.

10 Benazir Bhutto, *Reconciliation: Islam, Democracy, and the West* (New York: HarperCollins, 2008), 18.

11 Yousufi, interview.

12 Imam Zayn Al-Abidin, *The Psalms of Islam: Al-Sahifat Al-Sajjadiyya*, trans. William C. Chittick (London: The Muhammadi Trust of Great Britain and Northern Ireland, 1988), xv.

13 Sher Mehrani, personal interview with the author February 23, 2019, in Karachi, Pakistan.

14 Mehrani, interview.

15 Mehrani, interview.

16 Mehrani, interview.

17 Mehrani, interview.

18 Yousufi, interview.

6

Divergent Paths
Where Views Differ

Despite the many points of convergence between the Psalms and the Qur'an discussed in the previous chapter, some critical divergences also need to be addressed. Bashir Khan (pseudonym), a Muslim scholar and teacher in the department of social sciences at Lahore University, made this statement during one of my research interviews:

> If we are sitting and talking so that we only talk about the similarities, it is that I am not accepting and respecting [my] dialogue partner. . . . [Accepting both similarities and differences] has to be clear. If that [aspect] is not there, . . . it [dialogue] is a narcissistic self-affirmation; it is not a loving embrace of the one who is different from us.[1]

Responding to a question of whether the issue of doctrinal differences can facilitate conversation or dialogue, Professor Khan asserts, "Yes, it can facilitate the interfaith conversation. However, in the general principle of dialogue, our dialogues should not in any way minimize our differences. Because minimizing . . . or avoiding our differences would be a monologue, not a dialogue." It is understood that if we do not accept and live our differences, an entire dialogue is an exercise in futility.

We have already seen how Islam and Christianity diverge on the theology of musical worship: Islamic thought views music with suspicion, while Christians use music with boldness and theological integrity. Let us look at a few more areas of divergence.

Polemics: *Tahrif* and *Tabdil*

The Qur'an explicitly expresses a polemical context vis-à-vis Jews, Christians, and Arabian polytheists. Despite the pivotal link of divine revelation connecting the Qur'an and the Psalms, the first and foremost divergent aspect is a polemical stance of the Qur'an against Christians (Q Al-Baqarah 2:135–141; Q Ali Imran 3:64–71; and Q Al-Maidah 5:12–19, 78–86). These qur'anic statements are abstruse concerning the previous scriptures. At one point, the Qur'an affirms the tripartite division of the Judeo-Christian scriptures, endorses the divine source, and refers to it in the same revelatory chain of God's word. In contrast to this affirmation, the Qur'an also uses polemic language and accuses the Bible of *tahrif* (corruption) and *tabdil* (changes).[2] Muslims have charged Christians with copying and fabricating the previous manuscripts.

At the same time, the book of Psalms has generally been excluded from these allegations of change. While there are doctrinal divergences, the singers and scholars in my interview pool do not see any critical deviations concerning the Psalms in Islam.

There is a clear distinction between Islam's understanding of *wahi* (revelation) or *tanzil* ("sending down"; see Q Al-Isra 17:105) and Christian inspiration, which Muslim scholars put in a lesser category called *ilham*. According to the Islamic concept, the Qur'an is the final, authoritative, and authentic revelation of God in the continuation of Abrahamic religions. A Muslim-background believer states, "Muslim scholars told us that previous divine scriptures had been corrupted and changed; you cannot rely upon them."[3] That sole claim has worked to bar Muslims from reading or using the previous books. Due to the suspicious atmosphere surrounding these scriptures, the Tawrat, Zabur, and Injil have found no place in an Islamic canon; their contents mostly ignored and unknown to typical Muslims.

Philology: Arabic vs. Translation

The second main difference between the Psalms and the Qur'an is the nontranslatability of the Arabic Qur'an. Surah Al Shuara 26:195 describes the Qur'an as being sent down by Allah "in clear Arabic language." The revelation to Muhammad is described as coming from the divine source in this manner: "We have never sent a messenger except in the language of his people" (Q Ibrahim 14:4). The Arabic of the Qur'an is considered the verbatim of Allah, necessitating transmittal in the same arrangement (Q 12:2; 13:37; 16:103; 20:113; 41:3). Translations into the vernacular of other language cultures and ethnicities are considered inauthentic.

In contrast, the Psalms have been translated around the globe for the past two thousand years without the translations regarded as losing the power of divine and authoritative inspiration. The Damascus Psalm Fragment, with an Arabic translation of Psalm 78:20–31, 51–61, dates from the second century AH (After Hajj)—that is, the eighth or early ninth century CE—and is the oldest known specimen of Christian-Arabic literature. Abdallah ibn al-Fadl, a deacon of the Melkite Church in Antioch in the eleventh century, used manuscripts from the ninth and tenth centuries to produce and translate an Arabic version of the book of Psalms that became widely used in the Melkite Church. The Melkite community also produced various other parchments for the liturgy and scriptural readings. These manuscripts show that the book of Psalms was already being recited in Arabic prior to the ninth century for linguistic, liturgical, and learning purposes. Moreover, the Bukhari Hadiths give evidence that Muhammad and his companions had access to recitations of the biblical Psalms. Later ibn al-Fadl set out to provide a standardized and linguistically improved Arabic version of the Psalms.

The Reformer Martin Luther gave roughly equal importance to the original Hebrew, the Gallican Psalter (Latin), and Jerome's Hebraicum Psalter in translating his own German Psalter of 1524. Protestant insistence on the superiority of the vernacular for understanding and spiritual growth then led to the publishing phenomenon of the Genevan Psalter in 1562. Within the first two years, more than 27,000 copies of the Genevan Psalter were issued, and a couple of years later the publication reached 100,000 copies in over thirty editions, printed and translated in nine languages.[4] Onward from the sixteenth century, the influence of the Genevan Psalter on psalmody all over the world is impressive. The list of the translations of the Genevan Psalter—including French, Dutch, English, Hungarian, Indonesian, Korean, Japanese, and many more—affirms its global impact on the piety and scriptural singing of the Church worldwide. Moreover, the text of the Zabur is now available in Punjabi and Urdu.

Prophets and Messengers

The Qur'an and the Bible both paint a noble and honorable picture of the prophet and the concept of prophethood. In the Bible, *nabi* (Hebrew) means "spokesperson." In Islam, however, Muslims believe that prophets (*nabi*) and messenger/apostles (*Rasool*) are different offices. According to Islamic Hadith tradition, God has sent one hundred and twenty-four thousand prophets, but only four ranked as messengers and were gifted with books: Moses with Torah, David with Zabur, Jesus with Injil, and Muhammad with the Qur'an.

One issue of divergence in the Davidic dialogue with Islam concerns the innocence of a prophet. In Muslim theology, prophets are sinless (*ma'sum*), they cannot commit sin. The Qur'an (5:33; 4:59; 7:61), *Sahih Hadith*, and the consensus of the Ummah unanimously agree on *ismat*—the protection of a prophet from sin. The Qur'an denies and contradicts the very idea of prophets committing the worst of sins (idolatry, murder, adultery, and so on). Thus, despite the fallible nature of humans, the Qur'an defends prophets against slander and falsehood.

The Bible, on the other hand, counters this concept of the innocence of prophets and depicts them with human weakness and errors, despite their being separated or called/chosen by God for extraordinary office. We will take a deeper look at the similarities and differences between the Islamic and Christian views of the prophet David in a moment.

The Abrogation Theory

The Qur'an is not arranged in chronological order, nor is the Zabur. The qur'anic injunction mandated Muhammad's companions to transmit the current arrangements. Shehzad Saleem posits that *naskh*, the law of abrogation, surpasses the chronological sequence.[5]

The doctrine of abrogation is based on verses from within the Qur'an itself. For instance: "We do not abrogate any verse or cause it to be forgotten unless we substitute for it something better or similar; do you know that God has power over all things?" (Q Al-Baqarah 2:106). Also, "When we substitute one verse for another—and God knows best what He reveals—they say 'you are but a forger'" (Q Al-Nahl 16:101).

Farman Ali, a Muslim scholar in Lahore and one of my research interviewees, differentiates between Islamic tradition and Muslim thought. Muslim theology developed the abrogation theory in later centuries, allowing for flexibility in changing juridical rulings. Shehzad Saleem has said that Muslim thought discouraged the reading or recitation of other scriptures. These traditions have become famous among Muslims. As Saleem states, even those narrative traditions are proven inauthentic. Muslims mostly accept Hadiths very quickly without validation. However, because such narrated traditions spread widely, theologians accepted them and forwarded them from generation to generation.

Many in Islamic society listen to and take seriously pronouncements from the lower levels of interpretive sources (human scholars, jurists, and preachers) rather than the primary sources of the Qur'an, Hadith, and *sunnah* (the record of Muhammad's practices). At the same time, a noticeable trend has emerged among people engaged in Muslim-Christian dialogue for people from both faiths to read each other's scriptures and call for reasoning and interpretation based directly on the authoritative sources. Participants at the 2019 Interfaith Consultation in Lahore confessed that this trend has started very late because they have been told they should not read other scriptures and should focus on the Qur'an alone. However, people are now opening and reading others.

Regarding the value of a Muslim-Christian collaborative approach to the Psalms, honesty is the foundation of any interfaith relationship. Professor Bashir Khan excellently proposed, "Perhaps starting to bring Zabur with that angle [truthful interfaith dialogue] would create the environment of trust and comfort that is needed to discuss the more complicated issues. So, maybe starting with the Zabur would be the right place."[6]

David in the Qur'an and Hadith

What is the status of David in Islam? An examination of the convergences and divergences of the Psalms with the Qur'an is incomplete without considering the status of David (*Dawood*), the Hebrew king revered as a prophetic musician in each of the monotheistic Abrahamic faiths. In all three faiths, David is regarded as a prophet, praising God with his gift of a beautiful voice and musical instruments. We have seen in chapter 5 how both of the Islamic primary sources—Qur'an and Hadith—explicitly accept the Zabur as a divine revelation in the corpus of Muslim scripture. Both narratives describe David as an exemplary pattern for authentic prayer, piety, and penitence.

In the database resulting from my observations, questioning, and researched-focused interviewing, the respondents maintain that the Qur'an and Hadith present David as a model of gratitude and thankfulness. They use the Arabic form transliterated from the Hebrew *Dawood* instead of the Greek *Daud*. According to the Reference Qur'an 2016,[7] the name David is used in the Qur'an sixteen times (2:251; 4:163; 5:78; 6:84; 17:55; 21:78–80, 105–106; 27:15–16; 34:10–13; 38:17–26, 30). While the figure of David is crucial in linking Judaism, Christianity, and Islam, different understandings about David exist. In the Reference Qur'an, David is presented as a king of the united tribes of Israel, the father of Solomon, a prophet, and a poet.

Prophecy and Psalmody

In both the Qur'an and the Hadith, as well as in Sufi thought, *Dawood* is well known as a melodic singer and prophet who received the book of Zabur. Singing scripture is a prophetic ministry, and Islam affirms the link between prophecy and psalmody. Sufism provides the most explicit common ground between Muslim music culture and the role of *Dawood,* as a prophetic figure common to Judaism, Christianity, and Islam. He is revered for the power and beauty of his voice in uttering the word of God. The vocal instrument with which he was divinely endowed is considered in Islam the most beautiful voice ever created by God.

Ali al-Hujwiri (1009–1077), a Sufi buried in Lahore city in what is now Pakistan, described David's voice as so beautiful and enchanting that it attracted all manner of birds and wild beasts; it caused birds to fall from the sky, water to cease flowing, and enraptured listeners to perish, unaware of their need for food or water. God permitted *Iblis* (Satan) to "work his will and display his wiles" by playing instrumental music in order to distinguish the "followers of truth" from those who were merely slaves of their temperament. "The followers of the truth," wrote al-Hujwiri, "could perceive the divine source of David's voice and recognize the devil's music as a temptation."[8]

In the biblical narrative, David is esteemed for directing Israel in the worship of Yahweh through unconditional praise, praise resounding from every corner of the cosmos, Yahweh's macro-temple. In the biblical Psalter, David is known as Israel's musician and great psalmist, the anointed one of Yahweh, and the savior king. His significant achievement was leaving for Israel a prophetic hymnal for all times.

David's Wisdom

The Qur'an refers to David sharing wisdom with his son Solomon (Q Al-Naml 27:15). Additional verses refer to an occasion when David and Solomon together gave wise judgment for the damage caused by some sheep in a field, and directly following this reference, the Qur'an speaks of the worship led by David and involving the creation, including mountains and birds:

> And [mention] David and Solomon, when they judged concerning the field—when the sheep of a people overran it [at night], and We were witness to their judgment. And We gave understanding of the case to Solomon, and to each [of them] We gave judgment and knowledge. And We subjected the mountains to exalt [Us], along with David and [also] the birds. And We were doing [that]. (Q Al-Anbiya 21:78–79)

Another surah mentions a bountiful gift of wisdom granted to David:

> And We gave David bounty from Us: "O you mountains, echo God's praises with him, and you birds!" And We softened for him iron. . . . And to Solomon the wind; its morning course was a month's journey, and its evening course was a month's journey. . . . "Labor, O House of David, in thankfulness; for few indeed are those that are thankful among My servants." (Q Saba 34:10–13)

Both of these quoted passages speak of mountains worshiping. This figure of speech echoes Psalms 95:4, 98:8, 148:9, and other verses referring to the whole creation order praising God.

Another surah continues this theme:

> Be patient over what they say and remember Our servant, David, the possessor of strength; indeed, he was one who repeatedly turned back [to Allah]. Indeed, We subjected the mountains [to praise] with him, exalting [Allah] in the [late] afternoon and [after] sunrise. And the birds were assembled, all with him repeating [praises]. And We strengthened his kingdom and gave him wisdom and discernment in speech. (Q Sad 38:17–20)

The most significant point in this surah is the time of worship at evening and morning, carefully observing the order of day beginning at dusk. This story in Qur'an 38:17–26 tells about David judging between two plaintiffs who reached him by climbing over a wall while he was at prayer. This account conveys his worshipful heart even without him hearing the full case and it narrates David's repentance with the backdrop of his role as God's successor king and worship leader. The qur'anic reference in this story to the ninety-nine sheep whose owner demanded the one ewe belonging to his brother echoes the biblical story of Nathan's parable to David (2 Sam 12).

David as a Model Muslim Worshiper

Various Hadiths depict David as a singer, musician, warrior, and prophet. He is also an example of strict piety in Islam. Masudi (896–956), the Arab historian and geographer, believed that the building known as the Citadel or Tower of David in Jerusalem housed, at its highest point, the *Mihrab Dawood*, the place where David prostrated and worshiped. A Hadith narrates: "So David was one of those prophets whom Prophet [Muhammad] was ordered to follow. David prostrated, so Allah's Apostle [Muhammad] performed this prostration too" (Bukhari vol. 6, bk. 60, no. 331). Based on this Hadith, some scholars say that David was a real Muslim because he bowed in adoration.

After the *shahadah* and prayer, fasting is the third pillar of the Islamic faith. Hadith tradition says that fasting was to be a normal practice, like that of David. "Narrated by 'Abdullah bin 'Amr bin Al-'As . . . The Prophet said, 'Then fast like the fasting of David who used to fast on alternate days and would never flee from the battlefield on meeting the enemy'" (Bukhari vol. 3, bk. 31, no. 200).

Islamic researcher and scholar Rehan Yousufi commented,

> The Qur'an describes [David's] extraordinary ministry of a prophet who turns people toward God, and presents him as an exemplary *momin* [a man of God] and an excellent servant. His stories are narrated in the Qur'an, [showing him] as a person who is thankful to God, pious, God's favorite person. So the Qur'an gives him a special place. The qur'anic follower should respect and revere him as the Qur'an and Allah revere him.[9]

The Islamic Image of David

The discussion above about prophets and messengers pointed out the divergence between the standard Islamic view of prophets and the biblical view. Under the Muslim theological concept of *ismat*, prophets (including messengers) are considered sinless, innocent, immune from sin. In contrast, the Bible portrays prophets with a full range of human failings and weaknesses, giving a more nuanced portrait.

Islamic thought, however, is not monolithic. While Muslims universally acknowledge David as a prophet, contrasting views exist of his humanity concerning sin. Moreover, the Qur'an itself seems to allow for the possibility of prophets exhibiting fallibility (see Q Sad 38:24–25; 48:2).

In general, the Qur'an and Hadith present David's life as exemplary in Islamic prayer, piety, and practice. At the same time, some Islamic texts also portray his penitence and confession as a model for the faithful, conceding his vulnerability to flaws and sins. In particular, David Vishanoff's groundbreaking research, based in part upon original manuscripts preserved in European and American libraries, has uncovered various recensions and rewritings of the Islamic Psalms of David.[10] These texts, dating from the early thirteenth century, were created by Muslim scholars recomposing the Psalms for their purposes and understanding, rather than translating the original biblical text. One text presents David not only as an Islamic king but as a caliph (*khalīfa*), and also a proper Muslim prophet, because he receives a revealed Book from God that contains not human songs or prayers to God but God's direction, forewarnings, and reprimands to humankind. In contrast, because the Sufi form of Islam emphasizes God's grace in relenting toward humans, the Sufi editor presents David weeping over his sin and asking in frustration, "Can't the Devil use some other temptation than women?"

The primary audience of the Islamic Psalms are Muslims, not Christians or Jews. Different Muslim editors project the image of David for various purposes, reshaping the core text accordingly. Many manuscripts emphasize the enormity of David's immorality and sorrowful remorse, while others diminish his depravity and disseminate a piousness of austere belief and compliance. Each text adds a distinct tone and texture to the portrayal of David.

Vishanoff observes that Muslim scholars engage David to criticize the sins, preoccupations, or worldliness of the contemporaneous Muslim community, and to call Muslims to turn from their sins and lead a life of pious devotion to God. These editors were not preserving a sacred text but embarking on a literary venture analogous to writing the script of a sermon or collecting wisdom literature. David and his psalms were for them just a concept, a shared cultural source of convenient, modifiable material to convey their own beliefs about piousness. These findings provide historical evidence that the book of Psalms has been under the study of Muslim scholars for centuries and can serve as a common ground in Muslim-Christian engagement.

Reclaiming the Psalms as Powerful Witness

Despite divergences in views, the familiarity of David and the Psalms among Abrahamic faiths provides opportunity to initiate creative cultural engagement in Muslim contexts. Ghulam Abbas, a Muslim singer in Pakistan, has been recording and singing psalms and Christian gospel songs for the last four decades. He has numerous Christian students and is a famous artist in both commercial and faith circles. In 2019, I was invited to attend as a guest of honor at a musical evening in Karachi where Abbas was performing. I was permitted to conduct an interview with him while he was sitting on stage. He clearly stated, "Zabur is a book which has no contradiction from both Muslims and Christians. All Muslims believe in *Hazrat Dawood* [David] and Zabur."[11]

The status of David as a most respectable prophet and a pious king in Islam makes the topic of his legacy, including the book of Psalms/Zabur, approachable for Muslim-Christian dialogue. In particular, praise in the Psalms (for example, Psalm 136, a favorite among many Muslims) attracts Muslim scholars who appreciate and even sing David's psalms of thanksgiving. How much more progress can be made toward peaceful interfaith relationships if we determine more often to use the Psalms as a positive tool to approach the Muslim world. The power of the music and the prophetic authority of the Psalms in contemporary public witness and mission needs to be reclaimed for fruitful advance of the interfaith peace pilgrimage.

Notes

1 Bashir Khan (pseudonym), personal interview with the author February 19, 2019, in Lahore, Pakistan.

2 The general themes of these disputes include arguments over the nature of God (one or triune), Christology (human or divine), the crucifixion (fiction or fact), salvation (submission or redemption), the scriptures (corrupt or authentic, generally around Tawrat and Injil), Muhammad (true or false prophet), the Qur'an (miracle or forgery), various practices (e.g. polygyny or celibacy), and many more.

3 Haroon Ayub, personal interview with the author February 17, 2019, in Lahore, Pakistan.

4 John D. Witvliet, "The Spirituality of the Psalter: Metrical Psalms in Liturgy and Life in Calvin's Geneva," *Calvin Theological Journal* 32 (1997): 273–97.

5 See Shehzad Saleem, "Is Music Absolutely Forbidden?" (Al-Mawrid: A Foundation for Islamic Research and Education, February 20, 2015). http://www.al-mawrid.org/index.php/questions/view/is-music-absolutely-forbidden.

6 Khan, interview.

7 Safi Kaskas and David Hungerford, *The Qur'an with References to the Bible: A Contemporary Understanding* (Fairfax, VA: Bridges of Reconciliation, 2016).

8 Ali al-Hujwiri, *Kashf al-Mahjub (The Revelation of the Veiled) of Ali b. 'Uthman al-Jullabi Hujwiri: An Early Persian Treatise on Sufism*, trans. Reynold A. Nicholson (Cambridge, UK: Gibb Memorial Trust, 2000).

9 Rehan Yousufi, personal interview with the author February 20, 2019, in Karachi, Pakistan.

10 David R. Vishanoff , "Images of David in Several Muslim Rewritings of the Psalms" (Paper presented October 28, 2016, at conference "Warrior, Poet, Prophet and King: The Character of David in Judaism, Christianity and Islam," Warsaw, Poland: University of Warsaw, Institute of History). https://david.vishanoff.com/images-of-david/. See also "An Early Thirteenth-Century Recension of the Islamic Psalms of David: The Islamicized Style and Content of Istanbul Manuscript Fatih 28" (Paper presented April 28, 2017, at conference "Translators, copyists and interpreters: Jews, Christians and Muslims and the transmission of the Bible in Arabic in the Middle Ages," Córdoba, Spain: University of Córdoba, Casa Árabe). https://www.eea.csic.es/wp-content/uploads/2017/04/Programme-1.pdf

11 Ghulam Abbas, interview with the author on stage at a musical event March 2, 2019, in Karachi, Pakistan.

7

The Punjabi Psalter

The Legacy of a Century-Old Songbook

The Punjabi Psalter, originally published in 1908, has been called the "Bible of the Illiterate" in Pakistan. This first hymn book of Punjabi-speaking Christians in North India and Pakistan is a product of interfaith collaboration, and represents decades of painstaking planning and work. Its creators translated all 150 psalms from the Zabur into Punjabi lyrical poetry and then musically composed them in the Indian system of ragas, the region's cultural music. The subtitle of the *Punjabi Zabur: Desi Ragan Vich* ("in traditional ragas") reflects the significance of traditional ragas in the subcontinent music system, as discussed in chapter 3.

The story of the priceless Punjabi Psalter is God's story, and it is worth our attention.

An Anointed Translation

The book of Punjabi Psalms was born out of the mission of the United Presbyterian Church (US) and is the greatest gift given by Presbyterians to the Indian subcontinent. Most of the history of Muslim-Christian relationships in the North India/Pakistan region has been rooted in the fierce *manazra* model, featuring polemical encounters. Two historical debates—the Amristar debate in 1893 and the Agra debate in 1854—continue to be part and parcel of Muslim-Christian dialogue in the subcontinent. However, with the Presbyterian missionaries has come a different approach to interfaith collaboration.

The Presbyterian objective to translate and compose psalms in the native language was developed to sustain the religious life of both the missionaries and the converts. Until 1883, the worship community was totally dependent upon chants or a few metrical versions published in the book of *Zaboor aur Geet* (Psalms and Hymns) by other missions. But there were only a few pieces, and the text did not correspond very closely to the original scripture. Therefore, it was decided the Presbyterian mission should produce a separate worship resource. Before 1882, however, little progress was made, "partly because those interested in the work oscillated between the adoption of Eastern and Western meters."[1]

In 1882, the Presbyterian mission board commissioned a Psalm Committee to begin translating the book of Psalms into lyrical ethnic Punjabi language, with the first version in Western meter. An attempt was made to translate it into the Urdu language initially, but it did not succeed because the majority of converted people belonged to Punjabi ethnicity. The Psalm Committee decided to translate the Psalter into Punjabi lyrical poetry to provide a worship resource for these former Hindus.

Imam ul Din Shahbaz (1845–1921), a gifted poet and a convert from Islam who worked in an Anglican church, was appointed to translate the Psalms into poetic form based on Urdu, Persian, and English. The chairman of the Psalm Committee and others rendered assistance to confirm the exact meaning of the original Hebrew. Born in Zafarwaal, a United Presbyterian mission station in Pakistani Punjab, Shahbaz worked so hard that he lost his sight in the middle of the project. But his passion was so great that he continued with the help of a young companion, Babu Sadiq.

The Punjabi translations of the psalms were formed into 405 parts, all using the same meter (*dadra*: with six beats, 123 456; and *kehrwa*: with eight beats, 1234 1234). By October 1891, all 150 psalms had been published in Persian character, and subsequently they appeared in Roman script also. When Shahbaz's translation work was eventually compared with the Hebrew, it was found to be so excellent that it seemed God had given the psalms in the Punjabi language.

A Contextual Worship Resource

The next phase of the project was the musical composition of these lyrical psalms into native meters and melodies. It was found necessary to prepare versions of the *bhajan* form (a devotional song with a spiritual theme), and that too in Punjabi. As the translation work neared completion, the Presbyterian mission in 1890 appointed a new committee composed of all American missionaries, with the Rev. D. S. Lytle as chairman. Soon the committee realized that without native help they would be unable to finish the task. Long hours were spent in the marketplaces and cafés listening to current Indian tunes. The translator, Shahbaz, then paraphrased the psalms into Punjabi verse to fit the meter of these indigenous tunes. It was a contextual approach using familiar tone and rhythm patterns, and a monumental effort.

A Hindu musician named Radha Kishan composed the raga-based musical settings for the Punjabi Psalter, using many traditional or folk melodies. Most of the tunes were not treated as a musical interpretation of the text but were composed only for the sake of keeping the text.

The method of obtaining and adopting local tunes (public or folk raga-based songs) was initially opposed because of the original lyrics associated with those tunes. Some feared that people might remember the former "filthy words," which would prove detrimental to both worship and witness. Surprisingly, the former lyrics soon faded away from the memory of the people, and the worship community accepted the rich heritage of indigenous tunes set to the vibrant themes of the Psalms.

In 1893, an initial edition of the Psalter published fifty-five selections of psalms with music. Then the first full edition of the *Punjabi Zabur* was published in 1908 in Banaras, India—the first hymn book for Punjabi-speaking Christians in North India and Pakistan. The collection of 150 psalms included Western musical notation and Roman Punjabi script to help enable missionaries to sing along with local congregations. These Indian raga-based, *bhajan*-style psalms and Punjabi Sikh Gurbani Sangit, easily sung with traditional tabla and harmonium, become the power tool for both religious instruction in village congregations as well as evangelistic campaigns at *melas* (religious fairs) or in *bazars* (streets or squares where common business takes place and crowds assemble).

Robert Stewart, a missionary worker of the late nineteenth century, expressed his views about these *bhajan*-style psalms. After describing how the raga-based musical modes sometimes seemed out of tune to the Western ear, he continued:

> Yet some of its tunes are most delightful. Their very weirdness, wildness, plaintiveness and curious repetitions chain the attention and entrance the heart even of a foreigner, and to a native are as irresistible as the songs of paradise. Of some hill airs [ragas] introduced into a new edition of a Hindustani tune book, containing *bhajans* and *gazals*, the preface says, "Though monotonous in their endless repetitions, they are as weird and strange as their own Himalayas, breathing not only the sameness of mountain range, but the dash of streamlet and gleam of sunshine, or in the oft-recurring minors, the awe of unapproachable heights." Indeed, were it not for the popular songs which it has produced, Hinduism would be shorn of half its power.[2]

The Psalter's Legacy

As the first hymn book translated and composed in the Hindu-Muslim and Sikh context of the Indian subcontinent under British rule, the *Punjabi Zabur* offers creative space nurtured by United Presbyterian missionaries with the help and guidance of indigenous artists in contextual musical style. The Psalter's simple melodic tunes and lyrical texts help oral Christians to learn and sing them by heart.

The purpose of the Psalter's publication was theological rather than musical. Its focus was the accuracy of the text and the fervency of spirit. Thus, in translating the Psalms into lyrical Punjabi, like translating from Hebrew into metrical English, "the primary aim was a literal rendition of the meaning, while poetical form was of minor concern."[3] The strength of the United Presbyterian mission rested on preaching, education, and church planting. The Psalm Committee did not consider in what tones the pieces were sung, provided they were sung from the heart in the people's heart music and heart language.

Frederick Stock, a lifelong missionary to Pakistan in the mid-twentieth century, wrote of the *Punjabi Zabur*:

> It is difficult to estimate the spiritual impact of such a treasure of Scripture set to music and words readily understood and appreciated by the masses. Not only did it provide a medium for more meaningful worship, expressing praise, adoration, thanksgiving, confession, and consecration, but it was easily memorized Scripture with power to guard the heart from temptation and sin.[4]

Even after a century, no one has found any poetical or theological problems in these translations. Using the musical scales of indigenous ragas established a bulwark against an upsurge of Western hymnology and gave voice to local people to sing in their heart language and lyrics in the simple cadence of rote memory. The

Punjabi Psalter has been a successful endeavor to break the mold of Western Christianity, shaping Christian worship to be more relevant in the cultural and musical context of Pakistan. Moreover, the musical style and lyrical poetry reflect the qur'anic tradition of the Zabur.

Rather than continuing the theological and rational approach in the polemical *manazra* tradition in North India, the Punjabi Psalter is a product of interreligious cooperation that finds common roots in history and doctrine. The Punjabi Psalter is a major contribution to the body of material on church history in the Indian subcontinent as well as on the history of local creativity and cultural interfaith collaboration as the church approached the twenty-first century.

Presbyterian missionaries in the early twentieth century worked diligently teaching the tunes of the Punjabi Psalms to congregations, school children, and leaders in an oral tradition. These songs became an enormous blessing and a great aid in the growth, discipleship, worship, and witness of indigenous believers. Sadly, the societal prevalence of illiteracy and lack of native musical notation took their toll over time. By the time the generation who knew these tunes by heart passed away, the melodies of this Punjabi Psalter were gradually lost to use. The tradition of psalm singing declined until the present generation and has been largely replaced by modern, contemporary Pakistani hymns and songs. The current generation retains only 115 tunes in its current hymn book out of the original 405 pieces, and of these the worship community in the Indian subcontinent still sings perhaps no more than sixty to ninety of them. The rest of the 290 tunes have vanished from hymnals in Pakistan. Tehillim School of Church Music & Worship digitized the whole book of 150 Punjabi Psalms (1908) with the traditional Text and Tunes (Western Musical Notation). Available online at http://tehillimresources.com/.

The Siālkot Convention

In the midst of the Psalter's preparation for publication, a milestone event took place in Siālkot, a city in northeast Pakistani

Punjab. The Siālkot Convention in 1904 and the publication of the complete *Punjabi Zabur* four years later served and are still serving as catalysts for revival and renewal of Christians in Punjab.

In 1896, when General William Booth, founder of the Salvation Army, preached in various cities of Punjab, a wave of repentance and revival was ignited. This renewal also resulted in the formation of the Punjab Prayer Union (later called the Punjab Prayer and Praise Union), which invited Christian workers across North India to meet at Siālkot for a ten day Christian Life Convention. Prior to the convention, a whole month was dedicated to fervent prayer under the leadership of John Hyde, a North American Presbyterian missionary. Known as Praying Hyde, he had left the United States for India in 1892 to start a ministry at Siālkot. The prayer month was also led by McCheyne Patterson, George Turner of the Church of the Scotland, and Ihsan Ullah of the Anglican Church, who spent long hours on their knees in prayer. This spiritual movement gave birth to the 1904 Siālkot Convention.

This initial Siālkot Convention was unofficially convened as a pastors' conference to educate and equip newly converted worship leaders. By 1908, the first official Siālkot Convention was organized and became known as the "Mother of Conventions" in Pakistan. That same year the *Punjabi Zabur: Desi Ragan Vich* was published in Banaras, India. Ever since, the Siālkot Convention has been held each year during the last full week of September. The growth and the success of this convention seem to be linked with the use of the Punjabi Psalter.

The fire of the Siālkot Convention is kept burning by faithful generations. I had the privilege to design and lead the worship team at the convention for three consecutive years during my theological education from 1999 to 2002. The Siālkot Convention draws thousands each year, from villages and cities across Pakistan and even overseas, who come to reinvigorate their faith. It also has missional reach, as government officials and local Muslim neighbors witness the grace and providence of God through the sessions. The week-long convention provides food, fellowship, and worship in traditional and oriental styles, with indigenous music and heart songs in the native language of these worship communities. Preaching the Word of God is the heartbeat of this convention, and an expository book is published annually showcasing the biblical teaching offered in thirty-five services during the conference. The week of the Siālkot Convention ends with an early morning Sunday covenant renewal service with Holy Communion. People are sent out with the assurance of forgiveness to live a life as worshipers until their anticipated return the next year.

Prior to partition of the Indian subcontinent, the third wave of modern Protestant Christianity produced an indigenous Psalter and contextual creative models of spiritual resources that continue to have the strength to engage with common people on common ground in Pakistan. The book of Punjabi Psalms and the Siālkot Convention have brought sharp focus to the contemporary issues of renewal, revival, and witness of the church in Pakistan. These tools provide fresh channels to warm spiritually hungry hearts with God's holy fire. And, in the "Land of the Pure," what could be more needed than Pure Fire?

The Ongoing Potential of Music and Psalm Singing

My research and ministry have rediscovered the massive potential of using the Psalms in native text and tunes as the basis for Muslim-Christian interaction that results in a public witness.

As mentioned in chapter 1, Pakistan is a unique country where famous gospel singers are Muslim artists. In particular, performing and recording musical pieces from the common scripture of the Psalms/Zabur provides a natural bridge between the two faith traditions.

A Shi'a Muslim gospel singer, Ghulam Abbas, has been singing gospel songs since 1975. At a 2019 musical event in Karachi, he addressed the question of why he sings songs for Jesus:

> **Q.** Your name is Ghulam Abbas (a slave of Abbas), but you love Jesus—how do you justify this juxtaposition?
>
> **A.** I can justify that love does not have any religion. Love is love [audience applauds]. I could fall in love with any Hindu, Parsi, Muslim, but there is a reason why I loved him: The mystery in that love story is that he loved first [audience: "wah, wah," clapping].[5]

This response from a Muslim singer affirms that music surpasses all religious, racial, and ethnic boundaries and connects people's hearts and minds emotionally to each other. In the Pakistani context, musical genres and religious music generally allow Muslims and Christians to keep company and coexist peacefully. The musical gathering is the glue to keep people connected.

Music holds a mirror to all of life. From social to sacred, during the happy moments of a wedding or while mourning the loss of a loved one, through birth or harvest—all cycles of life are celebrated using similar musical language and lineage. As mentioned elsewhere, both Christian and Muslim music surfaced from the same Pakistani culture. Music is rooted in a historical process and provides an identity that leads to exploring the inner self.

Without question, Muslims and Christians follow and focus on different religious activities, and their worship methods and liturgical practices can be conflicting and even controversial. However, both faiths are nourished with the same musical pedagogy and practices in a shared musical heritage. Musicians have crossed religious worship boundaries. Two Muslim instrument players, a sitarist in Karachi and a clarinetist in Lahore, both developed "brotherhood with Christians," resulting in them attending and playing in Sunday worship services.[6] Christian religious songs and church music in Pakistan are also composed in the same cultural musical genres. Along with the Islamic months of Ramadan and Muharram, the Christmas and Lenten seasons produce an abundance of religious music, which is prepared and consumed by both faiths.

Musically, the popular genres of *ghazals* and *geet* are used for gospel singing. Sharing his own experience, Muhammad Ali, a celebrated Muslim gospel singer in Pakistan, says, "Ordinary people ask for *geet* [plainsong] type" during worship concerts.[7] He sees the purpose of the song from a spiritual and devotional perspective: "These are soul cleansing songs. The musical element should be according to the purpose of the song." Moreover, Ali admits that the "*qirat* [recitation] of the Qur'an [and a cappella gospel singing] are almost the same. The distinguishing [factor] is vocal embellishment with soulful melodic recitation."[8]

Nafees Ahmed Khan, the Muslim classical sitar maestro and music professor, also gave an example from his life. He gave his assurance that if his students were invited to participate in the Interfaith Psalm Festivals, he would love to send them with a cautious recommendation that "a music student come and observe this music and experience it. Though it is a part of Christian worship, nevertheless ponder on the music, as I have done: Why is it so powerful?"[9]

The only substantive element that separates sacred music from social is the text, which is based on scriptures or other religious literature. Muslims and Christians use the same musical language, but the text differentiates the purpose and meaning of a song. The religious texts of the Christian Punjabi Psalms as well as Muslim *naat*, *du'a*, *hamd*, *marsiya*, and Sufi *qawwali* are all composed in raga, based on the same music genres. The pursuit of both pure cultural music and the piety of religious music creates a musical space where Muslim, Christian, Hindu, and Sikh cross the threshold of their own religious identity and create a contextual interconnection through music culture.

There are a few caveats as well. Entertainment music culture has become a prominent influence on religious music in Pakistan. Even Muslim *naat-khwan* (*naat* singers) are adapting famous Indian film melodies for their religious music.[10] Muhammad Ali observes that commercial songs and rhythmic patterns are starting to dominate gospel songs, and says that *mujra* (a courtesan's dance, *bazaar Aang*) is also invading Christian worship music. Ali laments that many church music producers, musicians, and singers do not care about the Christian character in worship music ministry: "Reverence, honor, and purity are the missing components from the gospel/worship music in our generation."[11]

Common Ground and Collaboration

In sum, concerning the role of music culture and the common ground between Muslim and Christian musicianship, Dixon Wilson, a Christian audio engineer who has been working in the entertainment industry for three decades, concludes:

> In my opinion, the commonality between the Muslim and Christian religious music is that both talk about love, unity, living together peacefully, and respecting each other to work together. Both surfaced from the same culture. Christian and Muslim music is the same. Genres could be different. You may make a gospel *qawwali*, a rock-band style *geet*.[12]

Even the Urdu Bible translates the three main categories of musical genres noted in Ephesians 5:19 and Colossians 3:16 as *zabur*, *geet*, and Rohhani *ghazals* (psalms, hymns, and spiritual songs).

Dixon Wilson and other interviewees see the cultural, cognitive, emotive, and spiritual connection in Muslim-Christian relationships. Such collaborative gatherings foster friendship. Concerning the commonalities of the shared heritage and language of music in Pakistan, Nafees Ahmed Khan states, "Take this same music to a Sufi *mazar* [shrine], including the instruments, and people will use it in *qawwali*. Music will speak whatever they ask it to speak. Music is among those things that have been under human authority."[13]

According to my conversations with singers in this study, human beings have received music as a divine gift for meditation and to relax the human soul. Only the intentions of the human heart will cause people to decide whether they use music for good or for evil. Undoubtedly, as Nafees Ahmed says,

> The content of music is compelling and effective. It has a power that music can touch the heart, and if the poetry is for a good purpose. Moreover, if we move it this side, it gives us the same message, and if we turn to another side, it still gives us the same message.[14]

Another area for collaboration is connecting the Shi'a practice of mourning with Christian lament and the passion of Christ. The majority of Muslim gospel singers belongs to the Shi'a sect of Islam. The main reason behind this inclination is the Shi'a practice of *marsiya* and *noha-giri* (mourning). Both of the famous Muslim gospel singers mentioned earlier, Ghulam Abbas and Muhammad Ali, are Shi'a. Ali considers that the Christian "passion songs and *noha-giri* are the same thing."[15]

Significantly, Pakistan serves as a melting pot because of its famous Sufi shrines and its *qawwali* musical genre. The music culture of Pakistan is rich and robust for religious dialogue. Promoting peace through music is a daunting task, and Sufism has been at the frontline for more than five centuries on the Indian subcontinent. This notwithstanding, Christian singers in Pakistan are adapting the *qawwali* genres to communicate the Christian message.[16] Being reared in Pakistan as a Christian musician, I believe *qawwali* has the potential to promote peace and create a collaborative space for interfaith dialogue through shared musical heritage.

The Tehillim School and Psalm Festivals

Chapter 1 mentioned the Tehillim School of Church Music and Worship (TSCM) which I founded in 2003 (celebrating 20th anniversary in March 2023) under the approval of the executive board of the Presbyterian Church of Pakistan. This pioneering ministry center for worship, music, and interdisciplinary learning fosters the academic study of the ethnomusicology, missiology, and tradition of Christian worship in communities across Pakistan and the overseas diaspora. The school trains, equips, and promotes its students for contextually effective ministry with worship music that is both artistically and culturally relevant.

The Tehillim School (*tehillim* is the Hebrew word for psalms) has become a platform for learning and experimenting with psalms in Pakistan's missional engagement. TSCM nurtures and promotes an ecumenical spirit in the churches by providing training, workshops, consultations, and symposiums. Its goals include using performing art as a tool for mission and evangelism.

Among its activities, the Tehillim School has sponsored multiple worship symposiums and collaborative interfaith psalm festivals during which various passages from the Psalms/Zabur have been interpreted musically as well as through culturally meaningful choreography. At these events and on other occasions, I have had numerous opportunities to interview and engage in informal conversations with singers, musicians, and scholars about the Psalms and interfaith relationships. Muslim and Christian scholars have come to the Psalm festivals with similar themes and concepts from the Psalms/Zabur, providing significant scope for dialogue.

These interactions have yielded profound revelations. At a psalm festival in Karachi, I was able to meet a sitar maestro, and music professor Nafees Ahmed, who was invited to play on the stage. To my surprise, he played a famous tune in Punjabi from Psalm 22:27–31. In response to the question of where he learned the melody, he replied that while living in Rawalpindi, he used to attend church services with Christian friends. In addition, the 2019 Karachi Interfaith Psalm Festival featured a contemporary music band composed of Muslim and Christian artists who performed together. In the Pakistani context, the grandeur and professional level of the psalm and hymn singing is generally provided by Muslim singers, rather than Christians. This is a powerful collaborative approach.

In particular, I have gleaned many deep insights from visiting Sufi shrines as a participant observer and musical ethnographer in Pakistan. My 2012 visit to the shrine of Shah Abdul Latif Bhittai in Hala, Sindh, proved to be a landmark experience, opening doors for me to engage with Muslims throughout the country, including Sunni and Shi'a communities, about the role of psalms as a confluence in our faith traditions, aspiring to advance the goal of *salam/shalom*.

A Bridge for Peacebuilding

We have seen how Muslim music culture can lead to interfaith friendship, and how the texts and tunes of various religious music repertoires share common themes in Christian-Muslim conversations. The legacy of the *Punjabi Zabur* shows how culturally relevant songs with scriptural lyrics in the native language serve as a bridge for peacebuilding between Islam and Christianity. The drawn wisdom evoked by *qawwali* and other religious music genres rejuvenates relationships between both faith traditions.

The importance of using indigenous music and text for effective worship and outreach cannot be overstated. Pakistan's Punjabi Psalter could stand as a case study in efforts to decolonize musical worship. In colonized countries, some 90 percent of songs and musical styles used in the Christian community reflect remnants of a Western colonial mission. At The Hymn Society's centenary conference in July 2022 in Washington, DC, panelists described the English-language missionary songs as a parcel of colonialism in the Global South. The critical question for practitioners is how to decolonize tunes, text, and theological thinking to empower local congregations to engage in authentic local worship. In response to this question, the Indian subcontinent points back to the 1908 Punjabi Psalter, whose indigenous lyrics, rhythms, and raga-based music served to defend against Western musical invasion and enabled locals to connect with God in culturally meaningful ways.

Of all the books sent by the Almighty, the Psalms/Zabur holds unique characteristics as an eternal sacred spring expressing the most authentic relationship with God. If, as my respondents maintained, the Psalms are in fact considered by Muslims to be previous scriptures in a long tradition of revelation, then using the Zabur for interfaith friendship in a manner consistent with the Qur'an makes perfect sense. The application of scripture to daily ritual and life experience provides a means of relational convergence for Muslims and Christians in the context of living together peacefully in Pakistan.

Notes

1 Robert Stewart, *Life and Work in India* (Philadelphia, PA: Pearl Publishing Company, 1896), 303.

2 Stewart, *Life and Work in India*, 304, 306.

3 Wallace N. Jamison, *The United Presbyterian Story: A Centennial Study, 1858–1958* (Pittsburg, PA: The Geneva Press, 1958), 121.

4 Frederick Earl Stock, *Church Growth in West Pakistan with Special Emphasis upon the United Presbyterian Church* (Pasadena, CA: Fuller Theological Seminary, 1968).

5 Ghulam Abbas, in an interview with the author on stage at a musical event March 2, 2019, in Karachi, Pakistan.

6 Nafees Ahmed Khan, a Muslim classical sitar maestro and director of the music department of the National Academy of Performing Arts (NAPA) in Karachi, Pakistan, in a personal interview with the author March 1, 2019, in Karachi.

7 Muhammad Ali, personal interview with the author February 23, 2019, in Karachi, Pakistan.

8 Ali, interview.

9 Khan, interview.

10 Lekh Tandon, director. Produced by Shah Rukh Khan's Red Chillies Entertainment. Filmed on location in Darjeeling, India. https://www.youtube.com/watch?v=3KaYiEkcqKI. This *hamd/du'a* by a Sabri Qawwal is an adaptation of a song from the Bollywood film *Professor* (1962): https://www.youtube.com/watch?v=nOTxejJPvHY&list=RDnOTxejJPvHY&start_radio=1&t=1.

11 Ali, interview.

12 Dixon Wilson, personal interview with the author February 23, 2019, in Karachi, Pakistan.

13 Khan, interview.

14 Khan, interview.

15 Ali, interview.

16 See, for example, https://www.youtube.com/watch?v=epGRkL2Meql, with a recent Punjabi *qawwali* sung by a Christian *qawwali* singer.

Postlude
Taan

8

Psalms as a Mandate for Musical Mission to the Muslim World

The postlude of this book extends an invitation to the *pas de deux*—a dance for dialogue. Early Greek church fathers proposed the concept of *perichoresis* (literally "dance around") as a way to picture the inner life of the triune God. The early Byzantine fathers defined *perichoresis* as "The Great Dance . . . an image of profound peace in dynamic flow, of eternal give and take. The Persons of the Trinity are equal but different, each deferring to the other in the Love of the Great Dance."[1] Moreover, in the twentieth century, C. S. Lewis described this concept in his novel *Perelandra*:

> In the plan of the Great Dance plans without number interlock, and each movement becomes in its season the breaking into flower of the whole design to which all else has been directed. Thus each is equally at the centre and none are there by being equals, but some by giving place and some by receiving it, the small things by their smallness and the great by their greatness, and all the patterns linked and looped together by the unions of a kneeling with a sceptred love. Blessed be He![2]

Perichoresis resonates with the concept of *sur-sangam*, introduced in chapter 1: the confluence of text and tune in both singing and dancing that enables a gathering for the unity of souls and minds at one shared space. With this concluding coda, I welcome the reader to participate in the *missio Dei* (mission of God) and join the dancing circle of the triune God for interfaith dialogue with the Muslim world.

Music and the *Missio Dei*

Mission is a melody of God, and the Church is an instrument participating in the divine orchestra to bring forth songs of salvation. Over the past few decades, scholars have recognized mission as a major chord in the scriptural text, echoing the Church's identity and her witness to the world. The use of selective New Testament verses, such as the Great Commission in Matthew 28:18–20, often eclipses the mission mandate of the whole Scriptures, particularly the Old Covenant. Jesus himself opened the minds of his disciples to understand the fullness of the scriptures: "Everything must be fulfilled that is written about me in the Law of Moses, the Prophets, and the Psalms" (Luke 24:44). The whole of Scripture tells the story of God's mission—*missio Dei*—in the world.

While religious intolerance is properly documented, less consideration is offered to the process of counternarrative in the Islamic context and the resources available for the church to adopt. Pakistan is known to the world for religious extremism, sectarian conflict, and blasphemy laws. The influence of extremist Islamists has resulted in Pakistan's portrayal as a monolithic source of religious chauvinism. Most Westerners are surprised to learn that some 2.8 million Protestant Christians live in Pakistan. Through the lenses of a missional understanding of Scripture, I suggest that the Punjabi psalms composed in cultural music styles provide valuable understanding of the Pakistani missional imagination. Using the Psalms this way has benefits to both the contextual practice of mission and potentially theological education (specifically for preaching), as well as the witness of the worship community in Pakistan.

Peace is harder to keep than war. Many pivotal global meetings have emphasized the need for interreligious dialogue and cross-cultural engagement with Muslim neighbors—Cairo (1906), Edinburgh (1910), Lucknow (1911), Jerusalem (1928), Tambaram (1938), New Delhi (1961), WCC and Vatican Council II (1965), Berlin (1966), and Lausanne (1974, 1989, 2011)—with encouraging findings and direction. In aiming to explore the prominence of music in God's mission, my research helps lead us to discover the *missio Dei* among contemporary musicians in the Muslim context.

Missiologists and mission historians use the Latin term *missio Dei* to refer to the mission of God in the world. Based on John 20:21 ("as the Father has sent me, I also send you"), it means thinking mission in a theological way, where God rather than any human organization is a sending agency. In contrast, "mission" has commonly been viewed as an activity of the Western church and mission agencies from North Atlantic shores.

While the missional direction of God's story runs as a continuing theme through the Bible, mission is always contextual: it takes place in a particular time and space. How does the *missio Dei* help the worship community in Pakistan to develop a local missiology? How do theology and mission in Pakistan engage and investigate music in the twenty-first century?

For a biblical theology of mission in context, we must start with a missional hermeneutic—a way of reading and interpreting the Bible. A missional hermeneutic has the potential to provide a context and direction for preaching and teaching in Pakistan that connects the worship community for cultural witness with a bold and humble testimony. It also develops a new framework for learning missional practice in the Islamic context. Mission through worship as witness serves as a golden thread in the story of God, a dominant aspect of his eternal purpose, revealed throughout the whole biblical record and tying it together. Consequently, scriptures concerning the world must be read from God's perspective, and a missional hermeneutic will read Scripture with cultural and contextual sensitivity. In order to develop Pakistani mission praxis, we need to overcome the scientific polarization in Western hermeneutics, and we must be able to perceive and practice the overarching missional and spiritual hermeneutics found throughout Scripture and culture.

The testimony of the Bible reveals how God wants his people to bear witness to him, and thus we are not merely to partake in Christian worship but also to use worship as a witness. God's Spirit is inviting and leading the worship community to express his glory among the nations by engaging with their own respective cultures to praise as an exhibit to all peoples.

Music, art, and artists are on the frontiers of God's mission in the twenty-first century and play an integral role in creative missional approaches. Musical art from across cultures and with the religious Other can counter terror, create fraternity, and connect religious communities. For this reason, we need to understand theology through the lens of music and to provide a respectable space for music in theological conversation, which will, in turn, enrich our mission theology.

Music as Powerful Cultural Communication

Cultural anthropologists and linguists lead us to explore music as a communicative code. An effective communicator needs to learn to use such a code skillfully, for some messages are better conveyed through music than through other vehicles. Music powerfully engages the emotions as well as cognition and can serve to advance the *missio Dei*.

The historical roots of the Christian faith in the Indian subcontinent show the importance of this region in God's salvation plan. Missionaries used regular and irregular channels of social development, education, medicine, land ownership, and evangelism for mission purposes. The British colonialists established Christian presence by constructing cathedrals and Victorian-style church buildings. These nineteenth- and twentieth-century mission methods of education, social services, medicine, and an apologetical approach are no longer allowed.

In order to implement music as a theological method and the text of psalms as a cultural witness to Christ, the church in Pakistan needs to accept the rapidly changed missional paradigms in the twenty-first century. The major challenge is to unlearn traditional Western models and relearn cultural and creative approaches to engage the Muslim mind. J. Dudley Woodberry, dean emeritus and senior professor of Islamic studies at Fuller Theological Seminary, writes, "The Western Reformed Theology and the political-canonical Islam both failed to address the felt need of common people in spiritual encounters."[3] Muslim and Christian history has been eclipsed by philosophical, polemical, and political confrontation.

Researchers have long known that music is processed in different parts of the brain from speech alone. Don McCurry is a pioneering missionary statesman who served eighteen years in Pakistan between 1957 and 1975, then founded the Zwemer Institute of Muslims Studies as well as Ministries to Muslims. He tells a remarkable story about the power and utility of music to penetrate defenses, share biblical truth, and potentially advance the *missio Dei*. McCurry studied Urdu literature under Dr. Daud

Rahbar, a Pakistani scholar and Muslim-background believer with a musically well-trained voice. "Among all the valuable insights he shared," McCurry writes, "there was one that stood out from all the others. I don't know if Dr. Rahbar understood what a bombshell of an idea this was for a missionary. This is what he said, 'Don, you can say anything you want to a Muslim in poetry or music and he will receive it; but if you preach it in prose, he will probably try to kill you.'" McCurry goes on to tell how he put this assertion to the test while staging an International Music Festival in Murree and found it to be true.[4]

Imagining a Fourth "C"

Receptor-oriented communication of the gospel is a risky business. It requires that we go where the receptors are and identify with them in order to reach them (cf. 1 Cor 9:20–22). Nevertheless, recent signs of fresh activity at the music-theology-mission interface suggest that the difficulties are not insurmountable. I hope my research may serve to carry forward such initiatives, stimulating fresh and fruitful interaction.

In chapter 2, we examined what are sometimes called the three "C–encounters" reflecting the historical engagement of Christians and Muslims. These three "Cs"—Colloquium, Collaborative/Confrontational encounters, and Colonialism—have generally yielded minimal fruit over the centuries. More innovative creativity is needed to engage with Muslims in Pakistan using a doxological approach through music and the scriptural texts of the Psalms, in recognition of this incarnated Christianity.

For this reason, I propose a "fourth C": integrating "cultural texts (music) and Psalms" into the missiological context of Pakistan. Using vernacular translations of the Zabur composed in cultural music styles has shown how the Psalms has a powerful role to play in contemporary peacemaking possibilities.

After fourteen centuries of doctrinal confrontation, militant crusades, and colonial power plays, it is crucial for us now to seek creative alternatives in order to encourage Muslim-Christian friendships in Pakistan. New approaches need contextualized sensitivity, cultural relevance, and theological appeal to engage with the world of Islam. Reading, reciting, and singing the Psalms can provide an environment that overcomes fear and develops friendships with our Muslim neighbors. In the twenty-first century, missiologists are proposing new avenues for reaching out to Islam by engaging Islamic thought and expectations. Through an application of cultural texts (music) and the Psalms, I hope to move the role of the Zabur into the reality of contemporary peacemaking possibilities and seek to overcome the negativity of the historical clash between Islam and Christianity. This provides an inner voice within the cultural approach, allowing Christians to be better positioned to communicate the gospel within society and the public sphere around us.

Islam itself is not an obstruction to musical creativity; rather, it is scholars who have drawn lines on this subject. Indeed, many Muslims today display an ambivalent, elastic attitude toward music and popular culture, which, by mixing spiritual motifs with entertainment and popular lifestyle, is neither traditionally pious nor thoroughly secular. In Pakistan's soundscape, the social and the sacred can no longer be distinguished as being clearly different attitudes in the cultural discourse. The Muslim creative and cultural sphere is in a transition in the postmodern world, with simultaneous trends of both liberalism and traditionalism. On the other hand, traditional religious art forms are being marginalized and demonized. An emerging third option is the spirituality of musical art: a process of re-sacralizing musical art forms, immersing them with traditional Muslim values and symbolism.

Hope for Common Ground

Sociologists speak of the intersection of two cultures as creating a "third space" where something new and different can arise. The goal is to provide an alternative perspective rather than the historical tension, violence, oppression, and division that can arise from a clash of cultures. With a common concern for peace, understanding, and coexistence among persons of different faiths and spiritualities, those engaged in Muslim-Christian relationships through psalms aim to create an arena for prophetic, creative, and cultural dialogue. Religious identity is created on the juxtaposition of unity and separateness: honoring the dignity of difference while simultaneously promoting interdependence and respectful responsibility crossing the line of faith. This integrated, creative approach to dialogue offers an alternative position within the frames of the Muslim-Christian traditions.

Traditionally, the strategy to overcome religious differences has emphasized theological dialogue. However, the witness of the global Church needs to go beyond cognitive concepts. Despite the differences between Islam and Christianity, the shared spirituality of psalm singing allows us to communicate without violating each other's integrity, and to build a third space through creative Muslim-Christian conversations. This approach focuses on practical deeds uniting people on a spiritual level. Creativity, curiosity, and imagination arise as essential and intertwined elements of the Psalms approach to interreligious engagement. In the creative and practice-oriented processes of discussion within the field of music, empathy and imagination can enable participants to experience and gain insights that go beyond their religious repertoire.

Amidst widespread polemical practices and religious hostility, interfaith friendship and peacemaking are still very much prevalent in Pakistan, one of the world's most hostile countries for religious minorities. Here Christian and Muslim artists and academics build cultural and scriptural bridges with collaborative gatherings of *musicking*.[5] Particular emphasis needs to be put on praying and singing the Psalms as a common divine source, to show respect and love to our neighbors.

Creative and collaborative action structures play a crucial role in sustaining peacemaking for adherents of both faiths. The artistic and the academic communities provide a common heritage of music and an indigenous voice from the same soil, thereby creating emotional bonding between Muslims and Christians and religious harmony with those who share their experiences and network at the local and global levels. Despite the existence of theological and doctrinal divergences between Islam and Christianity, many of these differences are rooted in scriptural interpretation. However, the convergences of music culture and the concepts in the book of Psalms, with its secured and special status in Islam as Zabur, demonstrate how the religious similarities precede the polemical references.

The responses of my research participants reveal that references from the Qur'an and Hadith about the Zabur and its author, David, reinforce and stimulate the imagination about celebrating the shared heritage of divine song. These points of convergence foster peacebuilding between Islam and Christianity by unmuting the prophetic voice of David and the revelatory text of the Psalms for interfaith dialogue. Since David is a revered prophet of Islam, then the *sunnah* (practice to follow) of *Dawood* undoubtedly is to use vocal art for the praise of God.

In the Pakistani context, where religious tolerance is in an early stage, much water has streamed under the bridges, shattering religious harmony. The Zabur has a dual impact: one side is text and the other is tune. Music is such a vast and deeply felt phenomenon that connects to our soul and soil. Music provides us with a grounded and binding force, whether we sing from the Zabur or a Sufi *kalam* (devotional poetry), or simply want to connect. It will open windows to our minds and society as well.

From this perspective, the book of Psalms offers a distinct hermeneutic to bridge the Hebrew poetic genre of biblical psalms with the nonpoetic Qur'an. The book of Psalms parallels the Qur'an on five distinct levels, as we saw in chapter 5: Revelation (the prophetic and poetic origin), Recitation (the oral practice and transmission), Ritual (liturgical and canonical prayers), Reconciliation, and Relational convergences. The correlation of these aspects brings the adherents of both faiths to reimagine scriptural engagement using the common ground of the Psalms and the Qur'an as a catalyst to foster peacebuilding in the twenty-first century.

All these examples around the theme of *sur-sangam* resonate with the concept of *musicking*. The Psalms are close to both the Muslim and Christian heart. Based on the analysis of data that emerged from asking the research questions, we discover how the Psalms serve as a divine scriptural nexus between Christians and Muslims, with the commonality of parallel passages between the Qur'an and the Psalms contributing to peacemaking processes in Pakistan. Both faiths conceptualize divine revelation as well as the beliefs, values, feelings, and justifications associated with such truths. Understanding how one conceptualizes common ground involves an examination of beliefs, and the underlying feelings, about peacemaking.

Ideas and Strategies

Chapter 3 described the historic concept of *sangeet* in Indic musicality: the totality of vocalizing, dancing, and instrumentalization. The *sangeet* of Pakistan is rooted in the soil and expressed through the soul songs of the land. The church in Pakistan has powerful resources in the Psalms and their tunes. Such an approach is religiously authoritative and culturally authentic. The Psalms ignite artistic imagination and provide cultural awakening to communicate the Christian message. These opportunities suggest several ideas and strategies for Muslim-Christian engagement.

We have seen how interfaith psalm festivals provide a sturdy bridge to connect both traditions. The religious music genres in Pakistan are common to both Muslims and Christians and part of a shared musical heritage, making Muslim music culture a rich source for promoting peace. By using the divine text of the Psalms/Zabur, revered by both faiths and perceived by Muslims in the same monotheistic chain of divine revelation as the Qur'an, these interfaith festivals result in public witness through the scriptures.

In addition, when bands and worship teams at these festivals and similar collaborative public events include both Muslims and Christians, as occurred at the 2019 Interfaith Psalm Festival in Karachi, deep connections are formed. The theoretical framework of *musicking* suggests that music gatherings create a bond of unity between souls and minds in one shared space and lead to peacemaking and religious harmony. Although an attitude toward music may vary according to religious affiliation (that is, Muslim or Christian), the shared music heritage builds bonds between people of both faiths.

If King David is viewed as a prophet, then his work, the Zabur, can be treated in the piety model of revelation within Islamic thought. As such, it can be recited in the Islamic tradition of the Qur'an and thereby enjoys the heritage of sound and soil revered in Muslim thinking. In this way, then, the musical festivals committed to *musicking* the Zabur in Pakistan provide a strategic opportunity for peacemaking. As previously mentioned, almost every participant in my research study agreed that the Psalms can promote peace and friendship between people of the two faiths without theological or doctrinal alterations.

Psalms and indigenous poetic genres have striking cultural and religious parallelism in Pakistan, providing thick convergence points for engaging with Muslim neighbors through the religious poetic culture of Pakistan. Based on the rhythm, rhyme, and repetition in Hebrew poetry, it is easy to blend the linguistic and musical genres. The ideas and concepts of biblical poetry resonate with Pakistan's Eastern culture, with its oral and emotive poetic aspects. These convergences lead to cultural engagement that focuses on the poetic text and transmission of the Punjabi psalms using appropriate musical expressions.

A collaborative exploration of biblical psalms with cultural poetic genres will blend cultural concepts with spiritual spontaneity that expresses emotions reflective of *sur-sangam*. In 2016, Artesia City Indo-Pak church in Southern California, and then in 2022, Fresno Punjabi Fellowship in Central California, are the examples of Psalm singing principle yielding fruit. The house gathering service is attended by Punjabi Sikhs from India, and the most beautiful part of the service for them is the Punjabi psalms. Engaging the Psalms as one of the most profound works of the poetic genre with relevant musical genres will lead to transformations in both the affective and cognitive realms.

Specific Recommendations

> First, we need to read each other's scriptures. Secondly, Psalms are poetry, and Christians, along with Jewish faith communities, sing, recite, play, and pray Psalms. Thirdly, the Qur'an and Islamic understanding allow us to use creativity and art in our gatherings. These three things can create a common ground for peace and love in Pakistan.[6]

This quotation from my interview with Mufti Faysal Japanwala raises an important question: What are the best avenues to reach and engage an ordinary person in Pakistan? Educated elites and researchers argue from philosophical and theological perspectives, while peacemakers conduct dialogue, and apologists debate. Nevertheless, the original problem manifests when mobs come charging into the streets in the name of religion. How then can we reach the masses at the grassroots level? Based on this study, a few proposals are presented here.

Translation

To engage people at their heart level, the first area to pursue is translating the Punjabi Psalter into regional languages. Philologists state that over three hundred dialects are spoken in Pakistan, and each is distinctly different from the others. According to a 2017 paper by Agence France-Presse published in DAWN, a leading Pakistani news source, "Pakistan's 200 million people speak 72 provincial and regional tongues."[7] Each group deserves the Psalms in its respective heart language.

The Psalms have been composed in Punjabi but it is unlikely many people understand Punjabi. Here is a call for a massive effort to bring these sacred scriptures into the poetic forms of each language group so they can be used in musical outreach. Using the *Punjabi Zabur* as a basis for translation could prove helpful as compared to starting from scratch with whatever version of the Psalms currently exists in a language—and in many cases, these regional languages have little or no scripture translation to begin with. Pakistan's linguistic multiplicity prompts us to consider the value of translating texts and musically composing tunes in local music with modern instrumentation. Doing so will add fresh voices that provide access for the Psalms to engage in public places for missiological impact.

Regional Music

The second priority area for further study is regional folk music. Pensive regional music is rich and vibrant. Once I was teaching a course on worship and music at the Assemblies of God Bible School in the city of Quetta, on the northwest border near Iran and Afghanistan. A few Pashto-speaking Christian students composed a scripture song in their local language and music to present in a class. Such efforts could be readily extended.

The concept is to bring Muslim and Christian artists together, promote and spread the message of peace through music, and fill the religious gap using the bridge of the book of Psalms. Music influences emotions, and music is an intrinsic element of virtually every religious system. Cultural music practices that communicate at the heart level bring people together. Each music genre has its distinct expression that can play a significant role in peacemaking in Pakistan. Furthermore, musical *gharanas* in Pakistan and the inherited art of these musical families resonates with the history of the Levitical family and their musical duties in David's tabernacle and, later, in the Solomonic and postexilic temples.

Utilizing Music Genres

Utilizing multiple music genres, both religious and borrowed from film and other secular sources, can expand the reach of efforts to use music for bridge building. During the month of Ramadan, an abundance of religious music soars heavenward at the nighttime religious gatherings. Religious melodies and movie songs have had reciprocal influence on each other. Movies have borrowed famous Sufi *qawwali* songs and taken them to the entertainment arena, while religious singers also bring film songs into the religious realm. A particular *qawwali* singer in Faisalabad adapted the melody of the Indian movie song "Mere Mahboob Qayamat Hogi" from the Indian film *Mere Mahboob* (1963) and connected religious emotions to it by changing the text while keeping the tune.[8]

In particular, the Shi'a mourning tradition *Majlis-e-Marsiya* presents a vital aspect to uncover. As mentioned earlier, most of the professional arts community in general, and Muslim gospel singers in particular, belong to the Shi'a sect in Pakistan. Due to the emotional connection of mourning, the melodies of the Shi'a *marsiya* genre converge easily with narratives on the passion of Christ and the lament psalms.

Dance and Kinesthetic Aspects

Chapter 5 noted the convergences of the Psalms with Islam, including the similarity of ritual Islamic prayer postures with postures mentioned in the Psalms. Sheema Kermani, an Indian classical dance director, emphasizes that dance is deeply rooted in the subcontinent's cultural DNA. Even Christian scholars are recognizing the value of kinesthetic prayers and postures to interpretive singing.[9] Communal dance is an enthusiastic and exuberant expression. Sindhi Sufi *dhamal*, Rajhastan's *garbba* dance, and Punjabi *giddha* and *luddi* all exemplify cultural engagement through communal choreography at both social and sacred gatherings. In 2022, at the Global Psalm Festival in Artesia City, Southern California, a Hindu bharatanatyam female dancer first time performed on Psalm 139. The audience was stunned by watching and receiving psalms text interpreted by body postures and gestures. During field research at the Interfaith Psalm Festival in Karachi, Psalm 119:105–8 was choreographed and presented by Sunday school children.

Through simple movement and gesture, we can connect with the Psalms and embody what each expresses. The postures and poses help to convey the emotions found in the Psalms, and echo David's intent through cultural expression and interpretation as he danced before the Lord with all his might in the sight of his people (2 Sam 6:14).

Interfaith pilgrimage through the psalms using cultural choreography needs further exploration. King David often begins his psalms by addressing the choirmaster or leader. The psalms unmute the poets and invite participation from cultural choreographers. The *sangeet* and paradigm of psalm singing, instrumentalizing, and dancing provide an avalanche of God-given joy, as well as open access for interfaith dialogue.

The Role of Sufism

Sufism, as we have noted, is a movement within Islam offering a parallel path for spiritual expressions to adherents of all the major sects of Islam and beyond. Its contemplative and spiritual nature appeals to Muslims searching for a closer relationship with God. Music and spiritual dance play a prominent role in spiritual expression, paving the way to encountering ecstasy and experience ultimate reality. Drawing from such practices, prodigious North Indian music and vernacular Sufi poetry have created a hybrid musical genre, *qawwali,* that conjures the emotion of the divine presence in the human heart. The *qawwali* ritual arouses spiritual sensibilities. The esoteric concept constitutes the deep yearning and quest for ultimate reality via an artistic vehicle. Sufi music is a shared religious spectrum that brings people together for spiritual nourishment and interfaith relationships in Islamic contexts. The converging points of music and poetry connect diverse cultural contexts and serve as an avenue for spiritual pilgrimage.

A collaborative Muslim-Christian pilgrimage to Sufi shrines would present a symbol of walking together for peace. Such an endeavor would be an experiment to absorb the soundscape of the shrine. The message of Sufi poets and singers of the Indus Valley are addressed not to the rulers and scholars but to the farmers, fishermen, and nomads. These artists have built on a precious treasure of ancient folk legends and love stories everyone knows using vernacular languages and indigenous musical forms. In the Sufi mind, these legends acquired a new dimension as stories of the human soul on the path toward the Divine Beloved. The peacemaking potential of engaging with Sufi shrines, poetry, and music is waiting to be uncovered in Pakistan.

Collaborative Public Events

In addition to interfaith music festivals, discussed in more detail under the "Ideas and Strategies" on page 133, other kinds of collaborative public events present an area to explore. A participant in one of these events requested Muslim imams to bring students with beautiful voices to recite psalms in Arabic. This model also challenges Christians to consider learning the science of qur'anic recitation (*Ilm al-Tajwīd*). A variant of the annual Qur'an reciting competition could be adopted where young reciters of psalms are encouraged through gift prizes. In particular, youth and students need to engage in the peace process, including events arranged at a public place.

Salam alaikum – W'alaikum salam

Despite the differences in Muslim and Christian faith traditions, *Salam alaikum* (Peace be upon you) is the formal greeting used throughout Pakistan and a language of the three Abrahamic faiths, along with its response, *W'alaikum salam* (And unto you peace). The customs of peace greeting, whether *Peace!* or *Salam!* or *Shalom!*, include personal dimensions and communicative actions. At the interfaith psalm festivals, at conferences and interviews, every conversation and performance begins with the *Salam* to the audience. Peace is one of the primary motivators for interreligious dialogue and music can spread the message. Musical art is essential as a spiritual doorway to the religious Other. Artists regard the inner, spiritual dimension and the interpersonal encounter as the relevant scene for their creative peace message. Internal and external peace are closely related parts of human existence. Without peace in our hearts, we cannot attain peace with others.

One of the most significant challenges facing the global Church is addressing the need of people everywhere to live lives of wellbeing and wholeness—*shalom*. This book invites the whole Church to recapture a spiritual pilgrimage and walk together for the shalom of the nations. Creative and cultural forms foster Muslim-Christian dialogue in developing and deepening global interreligious relations. Peace is achieved through dialogue, and music is vital to this exchange. In light of the spiritual dimensions of the peacebuilding process, peace is not a question of rational decisions and considerations alone but about translating these cognitive commitments into feelings and actions. Musical art is regarded as an essential tool for contemporary peace striving, a conviction clearly mirrored in the planning and implementation of the interfaith psalm festivals and conferences.

Measuring the effects of music and psalm singing on interreligious relations is, of course, a difficult task. Nevertheless, the aim is to create sound spaces for cultural and spiritual encounters, conversations, and consideration by letting singers, scholars, and Sufis bring together their faith and music traditions in psalm singing interplay. The cultural context and religious settings allow for physical, emotional, and spiritual connections.

Therefore, the psalm-singing approach to the Muslim-Christian relationship should not be considered a replacement for solemn scholarly or theoretic efforts. A collaborative interfaith psalm festival can widen and deepen our creative imagination and appreciation of the multilayered phenomenon of Muslim-Christian relationships. The renewal of the heritage of divine songs expresses unity and vision for heavenly and earthly peace by using the text and tunes of psalms handed down through the oral traditions of the Indian subcontinent cultures. The power of the prophetic collaborative psalm festival aims to demonstrate that the reality of unified harmony is attainable and furthers the idea of peace—peace between people, between cultures, and within the nation, as well as inner spiritual peace with God.

Joining the Song that Never Ends

Psalms can play a significant role in peacemaking if we bring them into Muslim-Christian dialogue. Investigating the proposals suggested above and implementing them together with psalms can foster our combined spiritual pilgrimage toward peace. My prayer is that readers may use the findings of this study as a springboard for new research and applications in other missional venues.

According to the constitutional restrictions and national Islamic influence, Christians cannot use traditional methods of mission in Pakistan. Persecution generally happens as the result of witnessing but in Pakistan it happens because of religious hatred and faith-based social hostility. This study has explored Islam's extraordinarily rich cultural and artistic diversity, showing how sacred sound and religious music performance create a blend, a *sur-sangam,* to offer a window onto the subtleties and the humanity of the Islamic religious experience.

Devout Muslims pray five times a day for God to lead them to the "straight path" (*sirat-al-mustaqim*), the right path that is pleasing to God. Living peacefully with their neighbors is also part of fulfilling God's will and walking on a straight path in this world. Appealing to this spirituality with culturally relevant artistic expressions will find a wide audience. Furthermore, multicultural collaborative singing has a leading role in the book of Revelation (5:9–14; 7:9–12; and 15:3–4, for example), affirming the dominion of God and his ultimate purposes amid chaos and conflict. In contemplating and singing the Zabur, we join with Muslim neighbors to be formed in how we see God, ourselves, and the nations, both present and future.

There is a story of a villager in Pakistan who used a psalm to defend his faith. One day his landlord asked this poor, illiterate Christian worker a profound theological question: "Why do you Christians call Essa [Jesus] a Son of God?" Fearfully, but faithfully, the man responded, "I do not know why we call him that, but one thing I do know . . . ," and he then sang a simple, famous psalm in his heart language:

"Rahey Ga Naam, Sada Teekar Masih Da; Rahey Ga Jad Talak Suraj Rahega."

"May his [Christ's] name endure forever; may it continue as long as the sun" (Psalm 72:17, NIV).

Wa Allah ilm bilkhair—God knows best!

Notes

1 Darrow Miller, *Perichoresis: Great Dance of God and Creation,* http://darrowmillerandfriends.com/2018/07/16/perichoresis-great-dance-god-creation/

2 C. S. Lewis, *Perelandra*; p. 217 of the Macmillan Paperbacks Edition 1965.

3 J. Dudley Woodberry, "Power Ministry in Folk Islam," in *Encountering the World of Islam*, ed. Keith E. Swartley (Littleton, CO: BottomLine Media, 2014), 219.

4 Don McCurry, *Tales that Teach* (Colorado Springs CO: Ministries to Muslims, 2009), 81–84.

5 See, for example, "Dialogue of Peace," https://youtu.be/2Al4klNk2Xo.

6 Mufti Faysal Japanwala, personal interview with the author February 19, 2019, in Karachi, Pakistan.

7 *Pakistan's regional languages face looming extinction,* Dawn News, https://www.dawn.com/news/1306783#:~:text=Pakistan's%20200%20million%20people%20speak,%E2%80%9D%20or%20%E2%80%9Cnear%20extinction%E2%80%9D

8 Mere Mehboob [My Beloved], Harnam Singh Rawail, director, India: Rahul Theatre, https://www.facebook.com/voiceoftheheartofficial/videos/255977978922881/UzpfSTEwMTc3NTAzNTk6MTAyMTc5MDUyMjIwMzUwMTI/

9 See, for example, https://worship.calvin.edu/resources/resource-library/kinesthetic-prayer-an-example-with-the-prayer-for-the-holy-spirit-s-illuminatin-/.

Appendix

Parallel References of the Psalms and the Qur'an[1]

Qur'an/Surah	Verse	*Zabur*/Psalms	Comments
Bismillah al-Rahman al-Raheem	An opening invocation	Pss 103:8; 145:8	All 114 surahs (except #9) begin with same invocation.
1 Al-Fatiha [The Opening]	Q 1:2	Ps 25:4–6	
2 Al-Baqarah [The Cow]	Q 2:52, 57, 115, 116, 117, 125, 128, 131, 150, 152, 165, 173, 181, 182, 185, 186, 189, 199, 210, 213, 218, 226, 260, 284, 286	Pss 7:17; 24:8; 25:4–6; 27:1; 29:4; 33:9; 34:1–3; 34:4–5; 42:5; 44:21; 47:2; 50:15; 50:23; 55:22; 57:1–2; 84:7; 86:5; 89:11; 95:7–9; 103:8; 105:40; 116:1; 116:5; 120:1; 136:26; 139:4–6; 145:8	

continued

Qur'an/Surah	Verse	*Zabur*/Psalms	Comments
3 Al-'Imran [The Family of Imran]	Q 3:6, 10, 21, 29, 35, 47, 48, 59, 62, 96, 109, 129, 144, 152, 157, 165, 184, 185, 189, 191	Pss 139:13–16; 49:7–9; 39:11; 62:11; 5:3; 33:9; 93:4; 84:4–6; 89:11; 86:5; 57:9–11; 41:4; 116:15; 130:1–4; 147:5; 90:5–6; 89:11; 8:3–4; 19:1	
4 An-Nisa' [The Women]	Q 4:2, 11, 12, 23, 25, 36, 45, 58, 69, 96, 107, 122, 126, 132, 149	Pss 5:3; 8:3–4; 19:1; 33:9; 39:11; 41:4; 49:7–9; 57:9–11; 62:11; 84:4–6; 86:5; 89:11; 90:5–6; 93:4; 116:15; 130:1–4; 139:13–16; 147:5	
5 Al-Ma'ida [The Feast]	Q 5:3, 6, 34, 44, 54, 64, 74, 76, 95, 118, 120	Pss 5:4–5; 24:8; 27:1; 86:5; 89:11; 93:4; 115:4–7; 116:5; 119:1–5; 119:130; 130:4; 145:8	God is merciful; mighty; forgiving
6 Al-An'am [Livestock]	Q 6:2, 13, 14, 45, 54, 70, 73, 83, 96, 120, 143, 144, 145	Pss 4:3; 5:4–5; 19:12–13; 33:9; 44:21; 47:7; 49:7–8; 50:13; 65:3; 94:4; 103:3; 103:8; 139:16; 145:16	(Q 6:2 also cf. Ps 90:12) Forgiving; Most Merciful
7 Al-A'raf [The Heights]	Q 7:54, 55, 104, 128, 137, 153, 179, 200	Pss 5:3; 5:4–5; 5:12; 16:5–6; 24:1; 32:9; 47:2, 7; 116:5; 136:8–9	Merciful; All-Hearing

Qur'an/Surah	Verse	*Zabur*/Psalms	Comments
8 Al-Anfal [Spoils of War]	Q 8:9, 10, 11, 43, 52, 58, 63	Pss 5:4–5; 24:8; 39:7; 40:2; 44:21; 68:9; 68:17; 93:4	Powerful; Almighty
9 Al-Tawbah [Repentance]	Q 9:15, 27, 40, 59, 71, 72, 91, 98, 99, 111, 118, 124	Pss 5:3; 16:11; 24:8; 25:6–7; 32:5; 32:11; 33:13–15; 39:7; 65:3; 73:28; 93:4; 109:21; 116:5; 130:1–4	Forgiving; Merciful; Almighty
10 Yunus [The Prophet Jonah]	Q 10:3, 5, 18, 36, 43, 55, 58, 65, 68, 93, 94, 109	Pss 9:8; 32:11; 33:13–15; 44:21; 47:8; 89:11; 115:4–7; 119:160; 135:12; 138:8; 146:8	
11 Hud [The Prophet Hud]	Q 11:6, 7, 11, 90, 107	Pss 24:2; 27:14; 32:5–6; 115:3; 145:16	
12 Yusuf [The Prophet Joseph]	Q 12:64, 92	Pss 116:5; 145:8	Most Merciful
13 Ar-Ra'd [The Thunder]	Q 13:2, 3, 6, 30	Pss 19:2; 56:3–4; 65:3; 74:16; 116:5; 119:15–18; 123:1	Forgiveness and Merciful
14 Ibraheem [The Prophet Abraham]	Q 14:2, 8, 10, 18, 25, 36, 38, 39	Pss 1:3; 1:4; 18:1–3; 34:17; 65:3; 69:5; 89:11; 91:16	
15 Al-Hiijr [The Rocky Place]	Q 15:16, 20, 21, 56	Pss 19:1; 33:7; 42:11; 145:15–16	
16 Al-Nahal [The Bee]	Q 16:13, 18, 42, 61, 67, 78, 115	Pss 19:1; 103:8; 104:14–16; 130:3; 139:13–14; 143:8; 144:15	Merciful to All

continued

Qur'an/Surah	Verse	*Zabur*/Psalms	Comments
17 Al-Isra' [The Night Journey]	Q 17:1, 25, 30, 42, 44, 67, 74, 79	Pss 5:7–8; 9:7; 11:4; 47:8; 65:4; 107:23–28; 111:5; 119:62, 164; 145:8; 148:1–4	Merciful to All
18 Al-Kahf [The Cave]	Q 18:2, 15, 17, 27, 28, 46, 69	Pss 5:6; 19:9; 27:8; 39:7; 73:24; 73:28; 143:10	
19 Maryam [Mary]	Q 19:18, 35, 93	Pss 33:9; 119:91; 145:8	Merciful
20 Ta Ha [Ta Ha]	Q 20:5, 82, 89, 130	Pss 5:3; 65:3; 115:4–7; 103:19	Forgiving
21 Al-Anbiya' [The Prophets]	Q 21:20, 35, 79, 83, 112	Pss 11:4; 11:5; 30:12; 111:2–4; 148:9	Merciful to all
22 Al-Hajj [The Pilgrimage]	Q 22:5, 18, 31, 35, 37, 41, 54, 67, 78	Pss 1:4; 23:3; 25:10; 51:17; 62:11; 68:5; 78:52, 72; 114:7; 115:3; 139:13–16; 139:14; 150:5	Straight Path
23 Al-Mu'minun [The Believers]	Q 23:10, 14, 73, 118	Pss 23:3; 37:9; 103:1; 116:5; 139:13–14	Straight Path and Merciful
24 An-Nur [The Light]	Q 24:20, 35, 40, 46	Pss 23:3; 36:8–9; 116:5; 119:105	Straight Path; Guidance; Light
25 Al-Furgan [The Differentiator]	Q 25:3, 6, 70, 74	Pss 32:1–2; 65:3; 79:9; 115:4–7; 116:5; 128:3	Forgiving; Merciful
26 Ash-Shu'ara' [The Poets]	Q 26:9, 68, 71, 72, 81, 82, 84, 89, 159, 174, 217, 218	Pss 24:3–5; 78:32; 93:4; 101:2–3; 103:3; 103:4; 103:8; 115:4; 115:6; 139:2–3; 145:8	Merciful to All

Qur'an/Surah	Verse	*Zabur*/Psalms	Comments
27 An-Naml [The Ants]	Q 27:2, 6, 11, 46, 61, 63, 93	Pss 23:3; 24:1–2; 37:18; 65:3; 66:1–4; 103:8; 108:5; 119:105; 130:4	Guidance; Merciful; All-Knowing
28 Al-Qasas [The Stories]	Q 28:16, 73	Pss 9:1–2; 65:3; 103:8	Forgiving and Merciful
29 Al-'Ankabut [The Spider]	Q 29:3, 5, 17, 26, 42, 63, 69	Pss 4:3; 18:3; 24:8; 35:38; 44:21; 48:14; 66:10–12; 81:10; 93:4	All-Hearing; All-Knowing; Almighty
30 Ar-Rum [The Byzantines]	Q 30:5, 17, 25, 26, 27, 54	Pss 44:21; 66:1–4; 89:11; 93:4; 103:8; 119:89–90; 119:91; 145:8	All-Knowing; Almighty; Merciful
31 Luqman [Luqman]	Q 31:9, 18, 22, 27, 30, 32, 34	Pss 50:1; 62:7; 70:4; 78:32; 101:5; 107: 28–29; 139:13; 147:4	Almighty; Most Great
32 As-Sajdah [The Prostra-tion]	Q 32:6, 16	Pss 50:1; 119:62	The Almighty; Merciful
33 Al-Ahzab [The War Parties]	Q 33:3, 4, 24, 25	Pss 18:2; 23:3; 65:3; 71:16; 143:8	All-Strong; Almighty
34 Saba' [Sheba]	Q 34:3, 10, 27, 37	Pss 49:6–7; 89:8; 104:24; 139:16; 148:9, 10, 13	Almighty; The Wise
35 Fatir [The Creator/Pro-grammer]	Q 35:3, 5, 10, 11, 14, 25, 28, 30, 34, 38, 45	Pss 2:1–6; 18:30; 19:8; 34:22; 93:4; 105:5; 107:1; 135:17; 139:1–6; 139:13–15	Ever-Thankful; Almighty

continued

Qur'an/Surah	Verse	*Zabur*/Psalms	Comments
36 Ya Seen [Ya Sin]	Q 36:5, 22, 27, 52, 81, 82, 83	Pss 8:1–2; 33:9; 44:21; 57:1–2; 84:11; 130:4	Merciful
37 As-Saffat [The Ranks]	Q 37:159, 182	Pss 29:1; 47:7	
38 Saad [The Letter Saad]	Q 38:17, 18, 19	Pss 32:5; 148:9; 148:10, 13	
39 Az-Zumar [The Throngs]	Q 39:4, 5, 6, 9, 38, 47, 53, 63, 66, 67, 75	Pss 21:13; 33:18; 40:16; 47:9; 49:7–8; 88:1; 89:8; 89:11; 95:6–7; 104:19; 107:1–3; 115:4–8; 130:4; 139:12; 139:13–14; 150:1–6	Mercy-Giver; Almighty
40 Ghafir [The Forgiver (God)]	Q 40:2, 7, 8, 12, 19, 27, 55, 57, 61, 64, 67, 68	Pss 19:1; 33:9; 39:4; 41:4; 44:21; 47:2; 66:1–4; 106:8; 91:1–2; 103:1–2; 119:88; 139:13–16; 145:9; 147:5–6	
41 Fussilat [Made Clear]	Q 41:2, 15, 22, 30, 35, 36, 37	Pss 5:11; 32:11; 34:15; 44:21; 46:1; 93:4; 95:6; 145:8	Merciful to All
42 Ash-Shura [Consultation]	Q 42:4, 5, 12, 15, 19, 36, 51, 53	Pss 22:27; 29:2; 37:3–6; 47:2; 62:11; 89:11; 93:4; 147:5; 150:2	The Most High; Powerful; The Almighty; The Most Great

Qur'an/Surah	Verse	*Zabur*/Psalms	Comments
43 Az-Zukhruf [Ornaments]	Q 43:13, 19, 27, 45, 56, 80, 82	Pss 19:1; 89:11; 103:20; 111:14; 116:5; 136:15; 139:13; 147:5	The Merciful; Glory
44 Ad-Dukhan [Smoke]	Q 44:7, 20, 28, 42	Pss 18:2; 24:8; 55:22; 103:8; 136:21	The Almighty; The Merciful
45 Al-Jathiyah [Kneeling]	Q 45:2, 12, 27, 36, 37	Pss 24:8; 89:11; 106:48; 107:23; 148:13	The Almighty
46 Al-Ahqat [The Sand Dunes]	Q 46:2, 5, 8, 12, 13	Pss 93:4; 115:4–7; 116:5; 119:77; 139:23–24	The Merciful to All
48 Al-Fath [The Victory]	Q 48:2, 7, 14	Pss 25:4–6; 77:12; 89:11	The Almighty; The Straight Path
49 Al-Hujurat [The Private Rooms]	Q 49:1, 5, 12, 13, 14, 15	Pss 19:14; 44:21; 86:15; 111:4; 119:1–5	All Knowing; Merciful to All
51 Ath-Thariyat [The Scattering Wind]	Q 51:17, 18, 48, 50, 57, 58	Pss 5:3; 7:1; 50:12–13; 104:5; 119:62; 136:12; 136:25	Provider; Strong
52 At-Tur [The Mountain]	Q 52:28, 36	Pss 89:11; 116:5	The Merciful
53 An-Najm [The Star]	Q 53:31, 32, 62	Pss 19:12–13; 31:23; 89:11; 95:6; 103:12–14; 139:13–16	
54 Al-Qamar [The Moon]	Q 54:35	Ps. 75:1	

continued

Qur'an/Surah	Verse	*Zabur*/Psalms	Comments
55 Ar-Rahman [The Merciful to All]	Q 55:6, 19, 29	Pss 7:10–11; 8:3; 65:2–3; 104:9	
56 Al-Waqla'h [The Inevitable Calamity]	Q 56:3	Ps 75:7	
57 Al-Hadeed [The Iron]	Q 57:2, 4, 9, 15, 25	Pss 49:8; 89:11; 94:7–11; 116:5; 147:5	Powerful
58 Al-Mujadilah [The Dispute]	Q 58:1, 10, 17, 21	Pss 5:3; 49:7–9; 118:5–8; 147:5	All Powerful
59 Al-Hashr [The Gathering]	Q 59:1, 10, 22, 23, 24	Pss 24:8; 62:11; 91:1; 111:4; 116:5; 150:6	Mercy Giver; Powerful; Almighty
60 Al-Mumtahinah [The Woman Tested]	Q 60:1, 4, 5, 12	Pss 44:21; 62:7; 116:5; 143:8	Almighty; Forgiving; Merciful
61 As-Saaf [Solid Lines]	Q 61:1	Pss 19:1; 147:1; 150:6	Limitless Glory; Almighty
62 Al-Jumu'a [Friday]	Q 62:1	Ps 150:6	Limitless Glory
63 Al-Munafiqun [The Hypocrites]	Q 63:4, 7	Pss 50:9–12; 75:4	
64 At-Taghabun [Mutual Neglect]	Q 64:1, 4, 14, 17	Pss 44:21; 116:5; 145:17; 150:6;	Merciful; Limitless Glory
65 At-Talaq [The Divorce]	Q 65:3	Ps 138:8	
66 At-Tahreem [Prohibition]	Q 66:1	Ps 116:5	Merciful to All

Qur'an/Surah	Verse	*Zubur*/Psalms	Comments
67 Al-Mulk [The Sovereignty]	Q 67:3, 12, 29	Pss 116:5; 108:1–5; 143:8	Trust; Merciful
68 Al-Qalam [The Pen]	Q 68:32, 34	Pss 16:11; 37:34	Hope; Gardens of Delight
69 Al-Haaqah [The Hour of Truth]	Q 69:33	Ps 145:3	The Magnificent
70 Al-Ma'arij [The Gates of Ascent]	Q 70:33	Ps 15:3–4	
73 Al-Muz-zammil [The Enwrapped]	Q 73:8	Ps 37:5	
74 Al-Mud-daththir [The Enrobed]	Q 74:3, 31	Pss 24:10; 40:16	Glorify Great-ness
75 Al-Qlyamah [The Resurrec-tion]	Q 75:38	Ps 139:13–14	Created and Proportioned
76 Al-Insan [The Human Being]	Q 76:26	Ps 119:62, 160	
77 Al-Mursalat [Those Sent Forth]	Q 77:2, 21	Pss 104:4; 139:13–14	
78 An-Naba' [The Announce-ment]	Q 78:9, 10, 37	Pss 89:11; 104:23; 116:5; 127:2	Merciful to All
79 An-Nazi'at [The Forceful Chargers]	Q 79:32	Ps 65:6	
82 Al-Intifar [Torn Apart]	Q 82:8	Ps 139:13	He Assembled

continued

Qur'an/Surah	Verse	*Zabur*/Psalms	Comments
85 Al-Buruj [The Towering Constellations]	Q 85:8, 9, 10, 16, 20	Pss 7:12–13; 24:8; 89:11; 89:31–32; 135:6	The Almighty; Praiseworthy
86 At-Tariq [The Knocking Star]	Q 86:7	Ps 139:13	
88 Al-Ghashiyah [The Overwhelming Event]	Q 88:19, 20	Pss 65:6; 136:6	
89 Al-Fajr [Daybreak]	Q 89:28	Ps 116:7	
92 Al-Layl [The Night]	Q 92:6, 11	Pss 27:13; 49:7–8	
94 Ash-Sharh [The Relief]	Q 94:8	Ps 63:1–2	
106 Quraysh [Quraysh]	Q 106:4	Pss 46:1–2; 145:16	
114 An-Nas [Human Beings]	Q 114:1, 2	Pss ; 47:7; 59:16	

Note

1 Safi Kaskas and David Hungerford, *The Qur'an with References to the Bible: A Contemporary Understanding* (Fairfax, VA: Bridges of Reconciliation, 2016).